WONDERS OF MAN

VERSAILLES

by Christopher Hibbert

and the Editors
of the Newsweek Book Division

NEWSWEEK, New York

NEWSWEEK BOOK DIVISION

JOSEPH L. GARDNER   *Editor*

Janet Czarnetzki   *Art Director*

Edwin D. Bayrd, Jr.   *Associate Editor*
Laurie P. Phillips   *Picture Editor*
Eva Galan   *Assistant Editor*
Lynne H. Brown   *Copy Editor*
Russell Ash   *European Correspondent*

S. ARTHUR DEMBNER   *Publisher*

WONDERS OF MAN

MILTON GENDEL   *Consulting Editor*

Library of Congress Catalog Card No. 76-163363
© 1972—Arnoldo Mondadori Editore, S.p.A.

Title Page:
The glittering chandeliers, gilded woodwork, and blue velvet settees of the Opéra at Versailles bespeak the sumptuous court life of the ancien régime. *Against the walls, half chandeliers resting on mirrors are made whole by their reflections.*
Right:
A window of Louis XIV's chapel — bearing the distinctive double L reversed monogram of the Sun King — looks out across a courtyard to one of the wings of the royal château.

Contents

Introduction

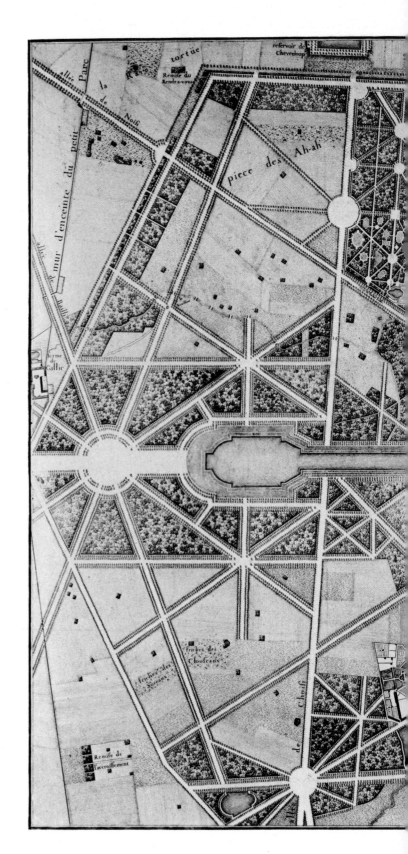

The Duc de Saint-Simon found Versailles "the gloomiest and most thankless of places; without view, without
woods, without water, without soil. . . ." The caustic
soldier and courtier was astonished that Louis XIV had
ever selected it as the site for his magnificent château —
the *maison de plaisance* of Louis's father transformed
into the seat of the French government. The Sun King
had succeeded in this ambitious task, Saint-Simon
wrote, by "tyrannizing over nature . . . subduing it by
force of art and money."

Louis was determined to make the palace complex
a grand enough symbol to awe his own nobility and to
affirm to all Europe that France's king was the most
powerful vicegerent of God on earth. But in spending
so lavishly on Versailles, he actually weakened the
foundations of his throne — and in willing to his successors his own propensity for extravagance, he virtually assured that the monarchy would ultimately be
brought to the abyss of revolution.

In the years after 1789 Versailles was first abandoned,
and then in 1837 transformed into a museum dedicated "to all the glories of France." But not until the
present century has it been restored to something like
its former grandeur — the exterior cleansed, many
rooms refurnished, gardens superbly replanted, fountain and fireworks displays held for the hordes that con-
firm its role as one of France's most popular tourist
attractions. And most of these visitors today would
probably agree not with Saint-Simon but with America's
Mark Twain, who was overwhelmed: "You gaze, and
stare, and try to understand that it is real, that it is
on the earth, that it is not the Garden of Eden. . . ."

THE EDITORS

On the 1746 map below the town of Versailles (right) surrounds the Place d'Armes, which funnels into the forecourt of the grand château. The gardens open out to the west (left), with the Trianon situated off the northern arm of the Grand Canal.

VERSAILLES
IN HISTORY

I

La Maison de Plaisance

One warm August evening in 1661, on a dusty country road in the île-de-France, an immense parade of carriages and horsemen could be seen approaching the great château of Vaux-le-Vicomte, thirty miles southeast of Paris. Nicolas Fouquet, Marquis de Belle-Isle and Comte de Melun et de Vaux, the Superintendent of Finance, had invited six thousand guests to what was to be one of the most magnificent and most momentous fetes in the history of France. Among the guests was the marquis's young master, King Louis XIV.

Louis was then twenty-three years old. Although he had already been king for eighteen years — his father, Louis XIII, had died when he was only five — it was not until the death earlier that year of his godfather, Cardinal Mazarin, that the young monarch had shown any inclination to rule his country himself. Until then Louis had appeared quite content to leave public affairs in the capable hands of Mazarin and the supervision of his private conduct in those of his mother, Queen Anne, daughter of King Philip III of Spain. On his deathbed Mazarin had urgently enjoined him to take up the government himself, to rule personally. "Govern!" the cardinal had said. "Govern! Let the politicians be your servants, never your masters." Above all he warned Louis against the presumptions and dangerous ambitions of the corrupt Superintendent of Finance, the enormously rich Marquis de Belle-Isle.

It was advice that Louis soon had shown himself eager to take. He had cried bitterly when told that the cardinal, whom both he and his mother had loved, was dead. However, he had quickly recovered himself sufficiently to inform the council in a firm voice, "In future I shall be my own chief minister."

The Marquis de Belle-Isle, who had expected to occupy that position, listened to these words with some concern, but he seems to have had no foreboding as to the fate that awaited him. Even when his brilliant assistant, Jean Baptiste Colbert, increased the king's suspicions that the marquis was defrauding the state of vast sums of money, Belle-Isle did not feel his future threatened. He was sure that the king would soon tire of personal government, would return to his hunting and his other pleasures, and would allow power to devolve upon the council, which he Belle-Isle controlled. As he waited at his splendid country estate to welcome the king and his other guests that August evening in 1661, the Marquis de Belle-Isle was looking forward to even greater riches and influence.

The château of Vaux-le-Vicomte had only just been completed. Designed by the greatest living French architect, Louis Le Vau, it was a building of dazzling grandeur. The interior, decorated by the paintings of Charles Le Brun, was furnished without regard to cost: rich hangings of velvet and cloth of gold were draped from floor to ceiling; thick Persian carpets rolled expansively from one stately room into the next; cascades of crystal shimmered overhead; scores of gold clocks stood on marble and porphyry chimneypieces, beneath graceful gilded mirrors; tapestries, specially designed and woven in a private workshop, were displayed upon the walls. In the gardens, laid out by André Lenôtre, were stone and gilded statues, glittering pools and waterfalls, lines of orange trees, and fountains between neat and vivid flower beds.

The king was at once delighted and infuriated by the spectacle. The ravishing beauty of the place could

This relief, and those introducing the following chapters, decorate the keystones of the ground floor windows of Versailles' western façade. They depict man's progress from childhood to old age.

not be denied, yet the money that had been lavished upon it was France's and his own. "Madame," he whispered to his mother, "shall we make these people disgorge?" He would have arrested the marquis that night had not the queen restrained him. "No, not in his own house," she cautioned him. "Not at an entertainment he is giving for you."

The entertainment was certainly superb. In the dining room the most favored guests were served with a light and delicious meal from silver plates; gold plates were reserved for the use of the king. Over the mantel there hung a portrait of Louis painted by Le Brun: the king admired it; the marquis immediately presented it to him. Other guests were presented with equally fine gifts, diamond tiaras, and even horses. After the meal they were all led outside to a theater, brilliantly illuminated by flaring torches that also lighted the fir trees and lawns. The king was invited to make a gesture indicating that he was ready for the performance to begin. He did so: immediately a sea nymph appeared from a shell; what had seemed before to be statues and trees began to move and to speak; satyrs and fauns danced out of the shadows. This charming surprise introduced a short *comédie-ballet, Les Fâcheux,* by Molière, and a dazzling display of fireworks set off to the sound of drums and trumpets. As the king walked back for supper to the château, the walls and windows of which were now illuminated by lanterns, hundreds of rockets shot into the sky above.

Few of his courtiers had ever before been treated to so dramatic and so resplendent a gala entertainment; few of them had ever seen so lovely a château as Vaux-le-Vicomte. As he rode back to Fontainebleau, Louis

was more than ever determined to bring down its presumptuous owner. He would also build an even more magnificent château for himself, employing the same architect, the same painter, the same landscape gardener. As to the site, he had already chosen it.

On the other side of Paris, in a sandy clearing in the woodlands between Saint-Germain and Fontainebleau, his father had built a small house to serve as a retreat for the night after a hard day's hunting. Over the years the brick and stone building had been enlarged: wings, designed by Philibert Le Roy, had been extended to the east to enclose a square courtyard on three sides; four pavilions had been added at each external corner; a moat had been dug; and small, formal gardens had been created. The château at Versailles-au-Val-de-Galie remained, however, an essentially modest country house, a *maison de plaisance,* with few large rooms other than a long drafty dormitory where the courtiers unwillingly slept. Unpretentious and inconspicuous, it looked far from regal in its sadly desolate surroundings of wild woodland, marsh, and fen. Indeed, neither the rather provisional-looking building nor the forlorn site contained much charm for most observers. Yet the young king was enchanted by the place. He felt the charm of its spell all the more strongly that summer of 1661 for he saw it through the eyes of a man in love.

He had been in love before but never so deeply as he was then with Louise de La Vallière. When he was seventeen he had become infatuated with the pretty little niece of Cardinal Mazarin, Marie Mancini, and had even wanted to marry her. But Queen Anne had heatedly condemned the match as unsuitable, and obedient to his duties as King of France, Louis had agreed to marry instead his first cousin Marie Thérèse, daughter of King Philip IV of Spain. He had agreed with a despairing heart, assuring Marie Mancini that, although he could not have her for his bride, it was she whom he loved and would always love. "You are the king," Marie replied, crying bitterly. "You love me, yet I must go away."

Louis was not much reassured by his first sight of Marie Thérèse. She was young and she had a good, clear white skin and hair so fair it was almost white; she had pleasant eyes and she looked kind. But she was distressingly stocky and not in the least good-looking, while her clothes and her hair style were as old-fashioned as they were unattractive. Marie Thérèse looked as though she might smell of mothballs. In addition, she spoke French haltingly with a heavy Spanish accent; she ate a great deal of garlic and chocolate flavored with cloves, which made her teeth black; and she had little conversation and no wit. She was very pious and thus was more at ease in the company of Spanish nuns than with the lively French courtiers. Also she was inordinately fond of her spoiled pet dogs and delighted in playing both with them and with the half-witted dwarfs that were usually to be found in her apartments at Fontainebleau.

Louis found his bride extremely boring. But he was a polite young man and he tried not to let her know, treating her, as a Spanish observer said, "with all the honors of her rank." She, for her part, was captivated by his charm, his strong body, and his handsome face.

Even his enemies agreed that Louis was a most attractive man. Some pointed knowingly to his prominent nose, maintaining that it looked Jewish; others to

The marriage in 1660 of the young King Louis XIV
to his cousin, the Infanta of Spain, is depicted in
this rich tapestry. Behind the bridegroom stands
Cardinal Mazarin, France's prime minister, who
arranged the profitable if not very loving alliance.

In the pastel below the artist Charles Le Brun portrayed King Louis at the height of his confident youth, his gaze firm, his hair falling luxuriantly over his shoulders. Le Brun had decorated the interior of Vaux-le-Vicomte (right), one of the most luxurious châteaux in all of France. When King Louis decided to build his own magnificent palace at Versailles, he looted the château not only of its riches but also of its artists: Le Brun, the architect Le Vau, and the gardener Lenôtre.

a somewhat Oriental aspect, assuring each other that he had — as he very likely did have — both Jewish and Moorish blood. He had in any case a finely proportioned face that commanded immediate attention and respect, and it was framed by flowing, curling brown hair, as beautiful as any woman's, which cascaded to his shoulders. Louis was tall and broad-shouldered and his back was very straight. He walked with exquisite grace. Women who looked at him often found it difficult to turn away until he disconcertingly returned their gaze through dark, mysterious, half-closed eyes. It was well known at court that he dutifully made love to his wife every other week and that each time, the next morning, glowing with pride, Marie Thérèse would take Holy Communion and pray for children.

Feeling that his marital responsibilities were fulfilled by these courteous semimonthly attentions, the king looked elsewhere for pleasure. And while looking, he unfortunately found himself attracted to Henrietta Anne, sister of King Charles II of England, who was married to his younger brother, Philippe, Duc d'Orléans, known at court as Monsieur. Philippe, who painted and powdered his face, colored his eyelashes black and did not wear a hat for fear lest he squash his exquisite wig, preferred the company of handsome young men to that of his wife and soon tired of making love to her. She, it was clear, had always preferred her brother-in-law Louis to her husband.

Since both their mothers naturally upbraided them when their attachment to each other grew dangerously close, Louis and Henrietta Anne decided that — if they were to continue seeing each other without arousing their parents' further anger — they must resort to de-

ception. Louis must pretend to be in love not with Henrietta Anne but with one of her ladies-in-waiting. The lady chosen to help them in their deceit was Louise de La Vallière.

The choice must have seemed a sensible one to Henrietta Anne, for Louise was not a noticeably attractive girl. She was rather awkward and self-effacing, she walked with a limp, and her face was slightly pock-marked. In the words of one of her rivals, she had "no bosom and few brains." But to Louis she proved irresistible. She was very feminine, which his wife certainly was not. She had beautiful big blue eyes, which often and unexpectedly filled with tears, lovely fair hair, and a pretty, sensual mouth. To Henrietta Anne's dismay, Louis fell in love with Louise. They went for long walks together; they spent hours alone together in secluded rooms; they went out riding together, where she showed Louis that, shy as she could be with men, she had no fear of horses, riding them without a saddle and even standing upright on their backs. Often they rode out together to Versailles-au-Val-de-Galie, and there they would eat *al fresco* meals in the forest and Louis would look at the small château and dream of the palace into which one day he would transform it. He thought too, perhaps, of the Marquis de Belle-Isle, arrested within a month of his splendid reception at Vaux-le-Vicomte, tried in the Arsenal on charges of treason and misappropriation of funds, and condemned to weary imprisonment in the fortress of Pignerol.

Louis plundered Vaux-le-Vicomte of its tapestries and furnishings, its chandeliers and ornaments, its statues and its orange trees. And he called into his service, as he had promised himself he would, those artists who

had bestowed upon the château its beauty and its grace.

Jean Baptiste Colbert, who had succeeded the Marquis de Belle-Isle as Superintendent of Finance and as the king's principal adviser, vainly strove to turn Louis's eyes away from Versailles. Partly he feared that the young and willful monarch would spend more than the already overstrained finances of the country could bear; mainly he considered that if money were to be spent on a grand new palace, the place to build it was Paris, where the Louvre could be extended and embellished to the greater glory of France. But Louis did not want to live in Paris, where the great nobles might get into mischief as they had done in his early years, the years of the civil wars known as the Fronde; he wanted to live out in the country. He agreed that the Louvre must be completed — but he would not live in it. Versailles was the place for him.

Colbert and his other advisers protested; Versailles was no site for a palace. As one of the king's courtiers was later to complain, it had neither view nor water, it was "all shifting sand and marsh." The walls of the original building had begun to slip almost as soon as they had risen above their insecure foundations. What might not happen when far greater weights were laid upon the drifting sand? In any case, the knoll on which the château stood was too small for a much larger building, while the site was too enclosed to permit an approach of any grandeur. "Oh, what a pity," Colbert argued, "that the greatest and most virtuous of kings should be measured by the scale of Versailles." Others pointed out that as well as lacking a distant view and water, the château had no nearby towns — the huddle of poor houses to the east being scarcely worthy

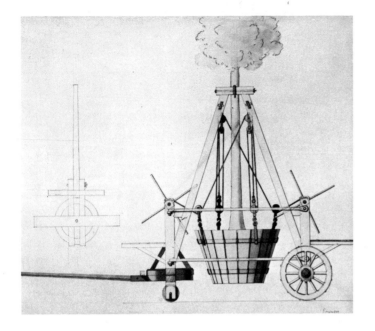

even of the name of village. Moreover, the marsh
would mean that the air would be unhealthy.

The king was unconvinced: marshes could be
drained, smart towns could be built, water could be
found, knolls could be enlarged, foundations could be
rendered firm. There was no distant view, to be sure,
but he liked the present limited one, which a compe-
tent landscape gardener could make much finer.

It was obvious that Louis's mind was made up, and it
had long since become clear to his ministers that once
the king had made up his mind there was little they
could do to change it. He would not even listen to their
suggestions that, if he really were determined to build
at Versailles, the present old-fashioned château ought
to be demolished and a fresh start made. He was unwilling to undo his father's work. That must stand; he
would use it as the core of his own new palace. Louis
Le Vau must find a way around every difficulty.

Le Vau certainly had experience enough; but Colbert's problem — money — remained. Thus, although
ambitious plans were drawn up, Louis perforce had to
be content at first with remodeling, redecoration, and
modest enlargements. Gradually, however, as the finances of the country improved, new buildings appeared. Two large, neat buildings of red brick and
stone, with dark blue slate roofs, were put up facing
each other across a handsome courtyard — to be known
as the Cour Royale — providing a smart new frame for
the entrance façade of the old château. In front of these
were placed two elegant and imposing entrance lodges
in the more ornate style of Le Roy's original building
behind them. These two lodges were joined by a row
of iron railings in the center of which was the main

entrance gate. Leading up to this gate, both from the
right and left, and sweeping past the lodges, were two
semicircular entrance drives on gently sloping ramps.
At the beginning of each drive, nicely positioned in
line with the lodges and the side wings of the château,
were two brick and stone obelisks surmounted by plain
stone balls.

Facing each other, across the open space in front of
the château known as the Place d'Armes, were built
three pairs of *pavillons* — commodious square brick
and stone houses with six large and three dormer windows on each front — for the accommodation of leading
noblemen and the actors, musicians, and other per-
formers who were called upon to provide the entertainments for the court. Behind these *pavillons,* on either
side of the château and to the west beyond it, Lenôtre's
men were put hard to work laying out the gardens, dig-
ging holes for the ponds, planting trees in neat rows,
making symmetrical beds for the king's flowers.

The king also loved orange trees — over a thousand
of them were taken from Vaux-le-Vicomte — and so
one of the gardens was a large orangery. This was built
beyond the south parterre, the Parterre des Fleurs, a
spacious garden court filled with all kinds of flowers
and surrounded by small cypress trees and shrubs and
a gilded balustrade lined with stone vases that were
painted to resemble porcelain.

Bright paint and gilding were to be seen on every
side, in striking contrast to the varying greens of the
surrounding woods and the warm red brick and bis-
cuit-colored stone of the buildings. The statues beside
the garden pools were painted in natural colors; the
iron railings along the front of the Cour Royale were

painted blue and gold; the balconies of the château were brightly gilded; even the chimneys and some of the cupolas were covered with a gilded copper that shone brilliantly in the sun.

Of all the garden buildings the most dazzling was the Grotte de Thétis, a single-story temple dedicated to the gods of the sea, facing the north walls of the château across the Parterre du Nord. The façade of the Grotte de Thétis was pierced by three large arches; at the top of the center arch was a gleaming medallion of Apollo, the Greek sun-god, a device that the king had made exclusively his own. Rays of sunlight, represented by thin golden bars, spread downward from Apollo's head, providing a grille for all three arches. Between the tops of the arches were circular medallions on which were depicted boys and dolphins playing together; and above these, on the parapet, Apollo was portrayed descending into the sea in his chariot, his day's work done. Inside the Grotte de Thétis, which was designed to represent an underwater cave with pebbles and shells encrusting the walls, were further representations of Apollo, his horses breathing fire, with tritons in attendance. The sound of running water fell upon the ear and from an organ in the south wall there came, with delightful incongruity, the chirping of hundreds of birds.

For those with less romantic tastes, the sound and sight of real birds were presented in the menagerie on the far side of the château, beside the road that led to Saint-Cyr. Here were kept hummingbirds and cockatoos, parrots and toucans, birds of paradise and lorikeets, flamingoes, pelicans, herons, and ostriches. The menagerie was housed in a sexagonal compound, walled and railed into segments around an elegant, octagonal central building, whose windows opened onto balconies from which the animals could be conveniently inspected. In addition to the birds, there were camels, leopards, lions, and two hefty elephants. Below the central building there was a cavernous grotto into which visitors ventured at their own risk, for pipes were concealed in the walls and floor, and by operating the appropriate taps the *farceur* could squirt the occupants with jets of ice-cold water. The king did not disdain this form of practical joking himself, and upon one occasion at least was observed turning the taps on and off.

It was clear to all how much the king was enjoying life in these early days of his power. He took immense interest in the alterations and new buildings at Versailles, riding over frequently from Saint-Germain or Fontainebleau to see how the work was progressing, asking how soon the buildings would be finished, going inside the château to inspect the ceilings newly painted by Errard and Coypel, then returning to his work and the pleasures of his court.

The queen, Louis had accepted, would never be exciting, but he was fond of her in his way. She gave him no trouble and bore him a son, Louis Le Grand Dauphin, later called Monseigneur, in 1661. Throughout Marie Thérèse's difficult labor, the king considerately held her hand. His mother, who was his wife's aunt as well as her mother-in-law, liked Marie Thérèse and was kind to her, and this made it the more easy for the king to enjoy the company of the sensual young Louise de La Vallière. It upset the king, however, that his mother, whom he deeply respected, so strongly disapproved of his liaison with Louise that for a time she would not speak to him, nor he to her. They took pains to avoid

one another, and one day, when by an unfortunate mischance they found a meeting inevitable in an empty salon, Louis merely bowed to her stiffly and walked through the door without a word. His mother burst into tears. "Ah, Molina!" she afterward cried to a Spanish lady-in-waiting, "Ah, Molina! These children!"

The king was as discreet as he could be; for the sake of his mother, he kept Louise in the background as much as possible, continued to treat his wife with every respect, and bestowed no rank upon his mistress — though he did accede to her numerous requests for court appointments and sinecures for her importunate relations. When Louise bore him children they were given no title and hurried out of the way to the care of Mme. Colbert. Once he did introduce Louise openly at court, sitting her down at a card table with his brother and his brother's wife, Henrietta Anne, but on that occasion both his wife and his mother were confined by illness to their rooms. Yet his mother, increasingly religious as she grew older, could not bring herself to overlook her son's immoral behavior; as the months passed, she thought it better to pretend that Louise de La Vallière did not exist.

Toward the end of 1665 the queen mother fell seriously ill; she had cancer of the breast and had not long to live. Louis, attentive and concerned, spent much of his time with her, even sleeping by her bed, while the doctors experimented with a variety of cures, many painful, all useless. One day, overcome by her suffering, Louis fainted. She died on January 20, 1666. In accordance with the custom of the time for royalty, her heart was sent in a silver box to the church of Val-du-Grâce, which had been built to celebrate Louis's birth,

her entrails were taken to the Carmelite convent in Paris, and her body was laid to rest in the abbey church of Saint-Denis, where a hundred masses were said for the peace of her soul.

The king went into the deepest mourning of purple and black, and walked about the court with sorrowful eyes. But he soon recovered his spirits. He had never yet felt the loss of anyone for long, and although he had undoubtedly loved his mother, her death was something of a release for him. His court was freed of her restricting presence; he himself was now wholly his own master, at liberty to regulate his life by no rules other than his own.

Soon after Queen Anne's death, Louise de La Vallière was created a duchess and officially recognized as *maîtresse déclarée;* their third child, Marie Anne, born that year — and the first to survive infancy — was declared legitimate. The queen gloomily protested, sulked, and said she would no longer sleep with the king. But Louis ignored her tearful protests, knowing that in her heart she still adored him and could easily be brought to heel like one of her own dogs.

In fact, as others in the court well knew, the queen had little reason to fear Louise de La Vallière of whom the king was obviously tiring. Louise recognized this herself and, in order to keep him amused when he came to visit her when she was unwell and out of sorts, she asked a friend, one of the queen's ladies-in-waiting, to join them. The lady could be relied upon to make the witty and clever remarks that Louise herself could never think of and which kept the king amused.

The friend was Françoise Athénaïs Rochechouart, the twenty-six-year-old wife of the Marquis de Montespan — as dark as Louise was fair, as sophisticated as she was ingenuous, as confident and self-assertive as she was diffident. Athénaïs was rather plump and voluptuous, sensual, and extremely ambitious. She was certainly far better looking than Louise; indeed, many found her beautiful. One contemporary judged her "the most ravishing, the most wise, the most charming of all the ladies at court." Another, the Duc d'Enghien, thought that "no one could have more wit or beauty than she." Her father was the Duc de Mortemart, Prince de Tonnay-Charente, the head of one of France's oldest families, whose members were renowned for their quick wit and inventive turns of phrase. The marquise's own conversation was a delight.

The king did not immediately warm to Athénaïs; he knew that she was trying to win him from her friend, and that she was flaunting her body and personality before him, as did so many other women about the court. He was surrounded by "female devils all seeking to tempt him," the Italian diplomat Primi Visconti said, and by fathers and mothers pushing their daughters forward for the sake of the power and riches that would come if he took them to bed. There was great honor in being the mistress of King Louis XIV; only the most devout considered such an affair a sin.

The Marquise de Montespan, though, was married; and the king's memory of his mother and her prayers for his moral welfare were still fresh in his mind. It was all very well for La Montespan to speak flippantly of her husband as a man of no concern; he *was* her husband and the father of her two children. She noted the king's unwilling admiration and reluctance. But she was content to wait; her self-confidence was not in the

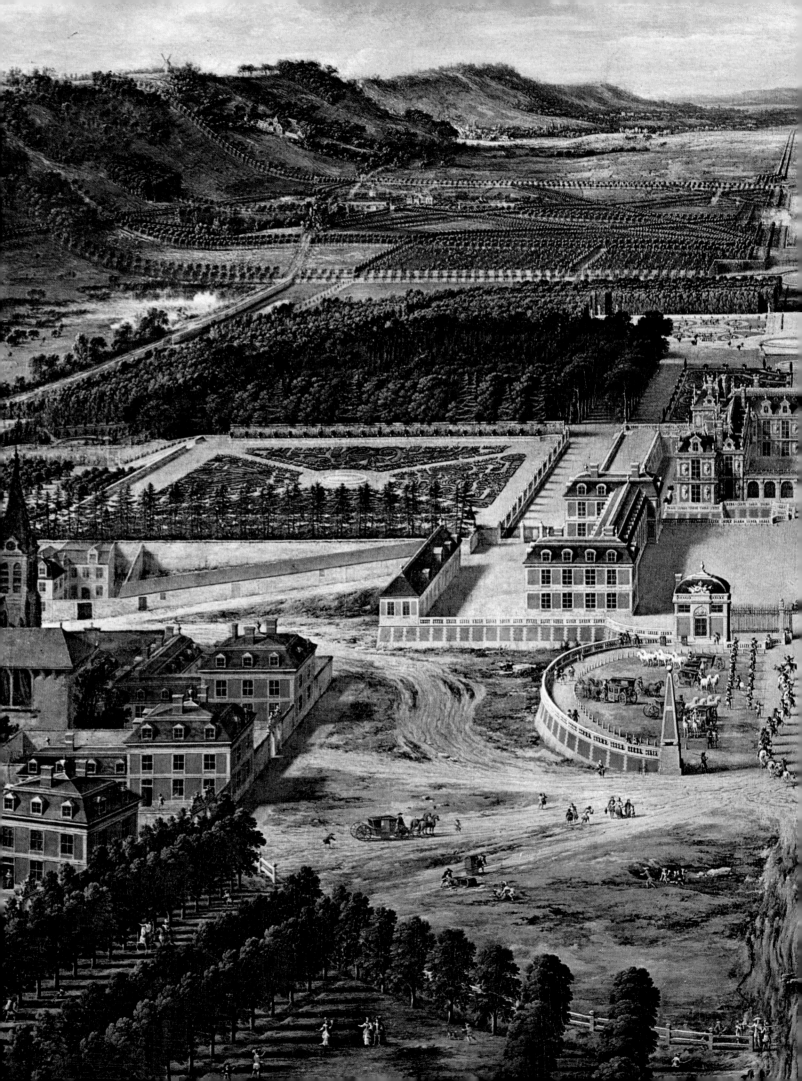

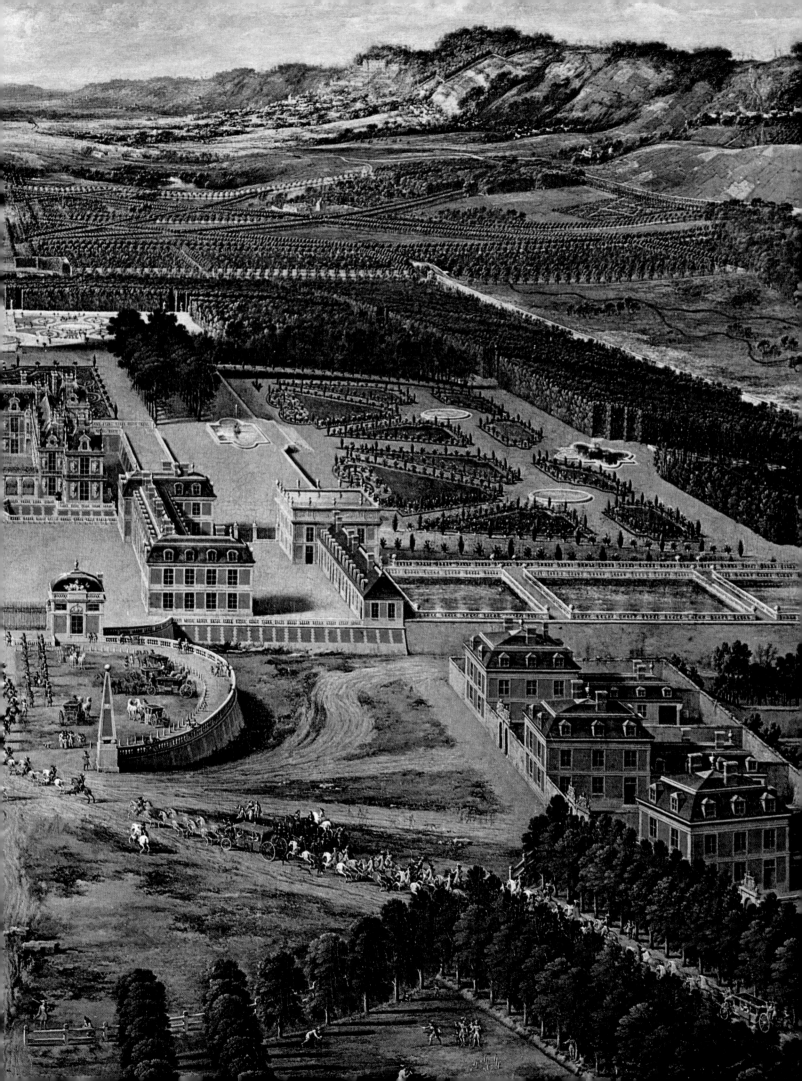

Seconde Journée
Theatre fait dans la mesme allée, sur lequel la Comédie, et le Ballet
de la Princesse d'Élide furent representée

least abashed. It was as though she knew that she would capture him in the end.

In May 1667 the king left Saint-Germain to join his army which was fighting to claim the Spanish Netherlands for France on the death of his father-in-law, King Philip IV. He took the queen with him, and, as one of her ladies-in-waiting, Mme. de Montespan. Louise de La Vallière, pregnant yet again, was left behind. She knew now that she had lost him; it seemed to her, so she said, that he had made her a duchess as he might have given a present to a servant upon retirement.

When he returned from the war, one of the king's first acts was to ride over to Versailles to inspect the new improvements. He wanted to see how well the gardens had been expanded and to make sure that they were fine enough for the grand fete he was planning to celebrate the victories that, concluded by the peace of Aix-la-Chapelle in 1668, had won extensive new territories for France. It was at this fete that the whole court learned of the king's love for Mme. de Montespan.

The king's first great fete, known as "The Pleasures of the Enchanted Island," had been held in the gardens at Versailles in the summer of 1664, when the passionate affair between Louis and Louise de La Vallière was still at its most intense. The entertainments, which lasted several days, were attended by more than six hundred guests, many of whom also took part in them. They were opened by an exhilarating fanfare of trumpets and the appearance of Louis himself — in gold, silver, and jewel-encrusted armor and a scarlet-plumed helmet — as Charlemagne's famous paladin Roger, who had come with his knights from their enchanted island to entertain the ladies of the court. Roger and his

knights, followed by Apollo in an immense and glittering chariot drawn by four horses and escorted by a multitude of elaborately costumed attendants, rode up and down before the admiring guests. The bright walls, blue roofs, and gilded chimneys of the château served as a backdrop to their skillful horsemanship in the afternoon light. The subsequent tournament, from which Louis gracefully retired, was won by Louise's brother, the Marquis de La Vallière, who was presented with the golden sword of honor by the queen. Then, after watching a charming ballet, the guests sat down to supper, which was served at long tables in the garden.

The next day the guests were treated to the performance of a new play by the great comic dramatist Molière, the first of whose *comédie-ballets, Les Fâcheux,* the king had so much admired at Vaux-le-Vicomte three years earlier.

Molière, whose real name was Jean Baptiste Poquelin, was then forty-two years old. He had been born in Paris, the son of an upholsterer who had done considerable business with the court. After some experience with his father's business, Molière had joined a troupe of actors whose success both on tour and in the capital was sadly limited. In 1658 the company nevertheless settled in Paris and was given a lease on a part of the Louvre known as the Théâtre du Petit-Bourbon by the king. Louis, while having a very low opinion of Molière's gifts as a tragic actor, rated him highly as a comedian and as a writer of comedies for his troupe. The king's faith in Molière's talents was soon confirmed by the production of a hilarious comedy of manners, *Les Précieuses Ridicules.* This success, of a wholly new type of comic play ridiculing the follies, vices, and ec-

centricities of French society, was followed by other triumphs — *L'École des Maris, L'École des Femmes* and the Vaux-le-Vicomte production of *Les Fâcheux.*

After the performance of *Les Fâcheux (The Bores),* the king had called Molière to him and said, indicating one of the most tiresome of his courtiers, whose long, involved, inconclusive, and banal hunting stories were notorious — "Why don't you put *him* into your play?" And Molière, who knew the man and his tedious manner well, obediently wrote him into subsequent versions of the farce. By then the friendship and understanding between Molière and the king had been fully established, and Louis had done his protégé the great honor of agreeing to be godfather to his first baby.

The opening play performed at Versailles during the summer fete of 1664 was *La Princesse d'Élide,* in which Molière himself scored a notable triumph as the idiotic valet Lycisas. But it was the subsequent first performance of an early version of his masterpiece *Le Tartuffe,* in the vestibule of the château, that was the highlight of the fete and established Molière's reputation as the leading comic writer of his time.

The fete also enhanced the reputation of another great artist to whom the king had offered his patronage. Jean Baptiste Lully, a composer of Italian parentage, had come as a child to Paris where he had worked as a scullery boy. He had first gained notice as a ballet dancer, but it was his skill as a musician that recommended him to the king, who appointed him master of his music as well as director of his operas.

Lully was an uncouth, ugly man, often drunk and always dirty, yet the king never failed in his high regard for him, affording the composer the same sort of protection that he afforded Molière, who was frequently in trouble with both the authorities and the bourgeoisie because of his satirical attacks upon their attitudes and conduct. Lully's music for Molière's *La Princesse d'Élide* and for a new ballet performed at Versailles the next day established him as the favorite composer of the court.

At the splendid Versailles fete that was held to celebrate the peace of 1668, the king once more called upon the genius of Molière and Lully to entertain his guests. Molière's new play, performed at the open-air theater in that part of the gardens known as the Allée de Saturne, was *Georges Dandin.* It was received with prolonged applause, as were the opera and ballet with music by Lully that were performed in the intervals. But so magnificent were the other entertainments provided by this *Grand Divertissement Royal* at Versailles in July 1668 that even the joys of Molière and Lully seemed to pale beside them in memory.

The *Divertissement* lasted but a single night, yet it cost over 100,000 livres, and even this sum did not include the expenses of the extravagant costumes provided for the guests. The fete began with a gentle promenade around the gardens, the new ponds, the flower-bedecked parterres, the *tapis vert,* across the Grotte de Thétis, and down to the lake. The gentlemen went on foot, the ladies in barouches. To refresh them on their way tables were spread with delicacies and the most exotic confections of marzipan, sugar, and *fruits cristallisés.* From the trees above them were hung fresh fruits, oranges, peaches, currants, and plums, which the guests could pick and nibble as they passed along. In a specially constructed building, the Salle de Verdure —

whose interior was decorated with garlands of leaves
and flowers, hundreds of candles, and rows of sparkling
fountains around the walls — the guests sat down to a
splendid supper at little silver tables. Afterward in another building, also specially constructed at immense
cost — its walls were of marble and porphyry — they
danced by candlelight or sat in private boxes ranged
around the floor, tier upon tier, to listen to the music
and to watch the beautifully dressed figures circling
around the floor below.

Before dawn broke, the company walked out into
the Petit Parc to see the walls of the château, as well as
the statues and trees in the garden and the water in
the pools, brilliantly illuminated by myriads of varicolored lights. Then, as a marvelously dramatic cli-
max, the whole black sky was suddenly irradiated by
the light of thousands of brilliant fireworks, while the
air was filled with the crash of exploding rockets. As
the last *feu d'artifice* burst into glittering light, the
king's cipher, the inverted L, was traced in golden and
silver stars above their heads.

The king himself, throughout the fete, had been at
his most charming. But Louise de La Vallière, who had
sat at his table at supper, pregnant for the last time, was
seen to be gloomy and silent and on the verge of tears.
Louis kept glancing across to the nearby table of the
Duchesse de Montausier, where the Marquise de Montespan, more beautiful and fascinating than ever, was
entertaining all those around her with lively shafts of
wit. No one who saw her, and who saw, too, the king's
small dark eyes repeatedly glancing toward her through
half-closed lids, could doubt that a new drama was un-
folding in the life of the court at Versailles.

II

A New Château Rises

No sooner had the last burned-out fireworks of the summer fete of 1668 been carted away from the parterres at Versailles, no sooner had the temporary buildings been dismantled and the gardens been returned to their immaculate neatness than the king gave orders for an entirely new château to take the place of the old.

The old château, handsome as it was and enlarged as it had been, was by no means commodious enough to house the ever-expanding court in even the most modest comfort for the shortest visits. Courtiers were constantly complaining of the cramped quarters in which they and their families had to live; many of them slept in garrets of which their servants would have had good cause to complain. When he learned of his master's determination to transform Versailles, Colbert once again endeavored to persuade him not to build there but in Paris. He used the familiar arguments that Versailles was no site for a great palace, that the king should live in his capital, the center of the civilized world, and he suggested that something could surely be made of the plans for finishing the Louvre that had been drawn up by Bernini.

Giovanni Lorenzo Bernini had come to France a few years earlier. His beautification of the piazza in front of Saint Peter's in Rome was admired all over Europe, and it had been hoped that he would be able to provide as fine a setting for the Louvre, as well as a noble façade. But Louis had not liked Bernini's plans; they did not seem to him to blend well with the surrounding buildings and were in any case too baroque. They might have suited Italy but not France. Unwilling to offend the great and haughty artist, Louis had allowed a foundation stone to be laid and had given orders for

the striking of a medal depicting Bernini's design. He had also granted Bernini an annual pension and had commissioned him to execute an equestrian statue of himself as a companion piece to the marble bust that he had carved while in France. Louis was highly pleased with the bust, which was generally agreed to be a masterpiece, but he deemed the equestrian statue — which arrived nearly twenty years later — execrable, and he banished it, after it had been altered to represent some Roman emperor, to a remote corner of the gardens at Versailles.

As for Bernini's plans for the Louvre, Louis declined to give them any further consideration. He would build at Versailles and there would be no more discussion of the matter. The only problem to be decided was whether to enlarge the existing château still further or to demolish it and begin all over again.

Various architects were asked to give their opinions, but eventually it was the designs of Le Vau, who had been responsible for the earlier work at Versailles, that were accepted. The plan was to envelop the Petit Château inside a new and grander one, to leave the east, or entrance, front as it was and to build around it, on the other three sides, a Château Neuf of stone, three stories high, with the roof hidden by a balustrade.

Once Le Vau's idea was accepted, work began in earnest under the ever-watchful eyes of the king. Frequently he walked out to inspect the progress of the work, to talk to the master masons, picking his way between the great piles of stones, the timber and scaffolding, the pillars, statues, and urns. When Louis could not go himself, he sent someone else to watch and report back; and even when he was away campaigning, he gave

orders for the fullest possible reports to be sent to him. Colbert doubted that the king, with all the other matters occupying his mind, could find time to study in much detail the accounts, drawings, estimates, and progress reports from Versailles, and he asked if he would prefer a resumé of them all. But Louis did not want a précis, he wanted long, informative dispatches, *"le detail de tout."*

Gradually, the new palace took shape. The magnificent west front, looking down across the beautifully arranged parterres toward the distant hills, comprised two identical wings — the king's apartments to the north, the queen's to the south — joined by an arcaded terrace that stretched all along the ground floor; the two floors above the terrace were deeply recessed between the wings. This front, as well as the new fronts to the north and south, was richly ornamented with statues, medallions, and reliefs, all artfully and symbolically contrived.

Along the western façade were bas-reliefs representing the twelve months of the year, each one placed above one of the first floor windows. Below them, and complementing them, on the keystones of the ground floor windows, were masks arranged in progression from the face of a child to that of an ancient man. On the south front, overlooking the parterre that led to the ramp of the orangery, were appropriate depictions of Chloris, the goddess of flowers, of her husband, Zephyrus, of Hyacinthus, whose perfect beauty so enchanted Apollo, and of other gods with whom flowers are associated. On the north front, facing the Grotte de Thétis and the reservoirs beyond it, were decorations, motifs, and statues connected with water and the

sea. And on the entrance front were emblems representing the four elements and thus the hospitality that the château afforded: air for the flying fowls, water for the swimming fish, earth for the produce that grew in its soil, and fire for cooking and preparing them all for service at the king's table.

On this eastern side of the château the offices were now incorporated into the main wings and, to render them worthy of the connection, their walls and windows were made more elaborate, and statues and balustrading were arranged along their parapets. Behind each block of offices was a pair of *pavillons,* ornamented in a similar way.

To make the approaches to the château more impressive three wide roads lined with trees were made to lead into the Place d'Armes. Meanwhile the small town of Versailles itself was entirely remodeled by Lenôtre, who set aside large plots of land, given by the king, to men rich enough to build suitably imposing houses upon them.

From one of these town houses a visitor to the château could walk down a wide avenue to the Place d'Armes and enter the Cour Royale through the open gate in the gold and blue railings that divided it from the town. He could then walk across this main outer courtyard, with the remodeled office buildings to his right and left, and mount the five shallow steps that took him into the inner courtyard, the Cour de Marbre, the original courtyard of the Petit Château, now paved with red, white, and black marble flagstones. In the middle of this marble courtyard was a fountain, the Fontaine des Enfants, which took its name from the figures of the little children that surrounded it. In the

The fountains of Latona (right) and Apollo (shown below and in detail at left) occupy the place of honor in the gardens of Versailles, along the axis of the château's main promenade. Apollo, god of the sun, the symbol of Louis XIV, is shown in his chariot, being drawn from the depths of the sea by his four chargers, that he may illuminate the heavens. Since the fountain requires more than a million gallons of water an hour, today it is turned on only infrequently. The fountain of Latona, Jupiter's mistress and by him the mother of Apollo and Diana, recalls the myth of the peasants who were turned into frogs for tormenting the goddess and her children.

courtyard's two westernmost corners were two wrought-iron and gilded domed aviaries in which numerous vividly colored birds swung on their perches and sang to the music of the water dripping and spraying into the basin of the fountain. Passing the Fontaine des Enfants the visitor then entered the château through a colonnade of red marble columns.

Coming out into the fresh air again on the far side, he would see a vastly enlarged and improved garden in which many fine new pieces of statuary of white marble or gilded lead by Marsy and Tubi, Girardon and Regnaudin had been placed at various commanding positions looking down across the park, back at the château, or facing each other over the *tapis vert*. The two main groups were of Apollo surging in his chariot from the waters of the lake and of Apollo's mother, Latona. As Jupiter's mistress, Latona was forced to flee from the anger of her lover's wife, Juno. When she paused to quench her thirst at a pool, Latona was prevented from drinking by a crowd of malignant country people who threw stones and handfuls of earth into the water by her face. She prayed to Jupiter for help and revenge, and he responded by turning her tormentors into frogs. In Marsy's depiction of this myth at Versailles, Latona is shown with her children looking toward the sky for help; around her are the tormentors — some already turned into frogs, spouting water into the basin; others on the point of metamorphosis. It was one of the king's favorite pieces of sculpture in the gardens; the lesson of vengeance wreaked on those who dared malign a royal mistress could not have gone unnoticed at Versailles. He often lingered by the statuary group as he took visitors on a tour of the gardens,

35

or paused by it as he walked toward one of the gondolas, gifts from the Republic of Venice, that carried passengers up and down the clear waters of the canal.

To some of those who watched the king gracefully walking around his gardens at Versailles — wearing, perhaps, a tall plumed hat and silk ribbons in his hair, an elaborate Venetian lace collar over an embroidered jerkin of blue and gold and silver, a knee-length coat of gold brocade enriched with little diamonds, red hose, and shoes ornamented with huge satin bows (their high heels a different color from the uppers and toes) — it seemed scarcely possible to believe that this elegant, refined gentleman worked eight hours a day and had, in the few years of his personal power, given the French nation new strength and power, a new sense of its purpose and destiny.

Louis had brilliant advisers, of course, but it was his own ambition and genius that had provided the driving force. In 1668, at the time of the *Grand Divertissement Royal*, when orders for the enlargement of the château were given, he was thirty and already the most formidable ruler in Europe. Successful in politics and war, determined and ruthless, glowing and vital, he did, indeed, epitomize *Le Roi Soleil* — the Sun King. Yet he was a sensual man as well as a hardworking one: he reveled in the luxuries of life; he loved rich materials and bright flowers, soft silks and scents. And the more he saw of her, the more he wanted to see of the Marquise de Montespan whose luscious white body a maid rubbed and massaged with scented oil for an hour or more almost every day.

The love affair between Louis and Athénaïs was far from being a peaceful one. Her husband, a violent and unbalanced soldier from Gascony, strongly resented the liaison. Occasionally he stormed into court, shouting insults at the queen's principal lady-in-waiting, whom he blamed for his wife's infidelity, or rampaging about his wife's bedroom and boxing her ears. Once at Bonnefort, as he rode through the main gateway of the castle of the dauphin's tutor, the Duc de Montausier, he shouted that he could not use the customary entrance as his horns were too high. And when he heard a rumor in March 1669 that his wife had given birth to the king's son, he announced that the Marquise de Montespan had died "from coquetry" and held a mock funeral, thereafter draping himself and his carriage in heavy mourning.

Eventually the king was able to silence the embarrassing outbursts of the marquis only by having him imprisoned and then banished to his remote estates. The offense, conveniently, was not directly related to his fury at his wife's adultery. He had seduced a peasant girl, given her a soldier's uniform, and enlisted her in his regiment. A bailiff had rescued her, at her family's instigation, and had locked her up in a prison to keep her out of the marquis's clutches. Montespan, thereupon, had stormed the bailiff's house with his troops, dragged the poor man out, and severely beaten him.

Although it was clear to her, as it was to everyone else, that she had lost all power to attract the king, Louise de La Vallière still remained at court, tearful and lonely. She still loved Louis and hoped that perhaps she might win him back. Patiently she endured the humiliation of his walking through her apartments to reach those of La Montespan. Louise's hope was sadly forlorn. Her rival grew bolder, more confident

every day, as the king fell more and more deeply in love with her. Knowing that her royal lover preferred fair hair to dark, Athénaïs dyed her own and arranged it in a new style that soon became fashionable — and was even copied by the queen, who pathetically apologized to her for doing so but hoped that she might be excused on the grounds that it was a style her adored husband so obviously liked.

Then Louise de La Vallière fell ill. It was thought for a time that she might die, and in her fear of death her thoughts turned to God. Upon her recovery she did for a time go into a convent from which she returned to court at the king's half-hearted request. But she was now miserable at court. She discussed her dilemma at length with the priests of the king's chapel; she fasted; she slept on the floor; she went so far as to wear a hair shirt. At last the call came, and Louise went to the king to ask for permission to enter the religious life. He looked upon her faded charms and gave his consent.

As a parting gift for the two living children she had borne for Louis, she had herself painted in the posture of a woman rejecting the pleasures of the world — represented by jewels, cards, a guitar, and a mask — and preparing herself for her new vocation. She publicly begged forgiveness of the queen, and the next morning she was driven to the strictest convent in all Paris, where her hair was cut off and where she put on the brown serge habit of the Carmelites. Louise de La Vallière, Duchesse de Voucars, became Sister Louise de La Miséricorde.

With Louise's departure, the Marquise de Montespan's position at court was indisputably established. Ministers consulted her; foreign envoys presented her with expensive gifts; and she ensured that she received even more valuable presents from her lover, who seemed able to deny her nothing. She asked for fewer profitable appointments and sinecures for her friends and relations than her predecessor had done, but this was merely because she had fewer people whom she wished to gratify. Indeed, she appeared to take peculiar delight in humiliating the importunate with her ready and devastating wit. Her arrogance was stupendous; her extravagance, astounding. She gambled for enormous stakes, once losing the equivalent of $100,000 in the course of a single day. The queen, who had got on well enough with Louise de La Vallière, could not abide Athénaïs. Yet the king continued to adore her, praising her courage and her resilience — when she insisted on accompanying him on his uncomfortable campaigns though in an advanced state of pregnancy — and lavishing his time and money upon her with equal unconcern for the value of either.

In order to be able to spend more time alone in her delightful company, Louis ordered Le Vau and Lenôtre to build a little château, a kind of elaborate summerhouse with its own private garden, in a remote part of the grounds at Versailles. The site chosen for this secluded retreat was on the outskirts of the little village of Trianon, which stood at the end of one of the branches of the canal that had been extended to the west of the château the year before. Work began there in the autumn of 1669.

Le Vau died before the work was finished and was succeeded by François Dorbay; but it was Le Vau who was responsible for its ultimate appearance. That appearance was not exactly as the king had intended it.

The king had envisaged a pavilion in the Chinese style that was just becoming fashionable. The Porcelain Tower at the palace of the great Emperor K'ang-hsi in Nanking had recently come to the notice of European art patrons and architects; and it was in a representation of this that Louis pictured himself entertaining the Marquise de Montespan. Le Vau had other ideas: he envisioned a more classical, Italianate building. But in deference to the king's wishes, the architect agreed to ornament the lines of his well-ordered façades with blue and white motifs, porcelain tiles and urns, and representations of birds. He also had the wooden casements of the windows, the statues in the gardens, and the vases along the top of the garden wall all painted to resemble porcelain. The same delicate and intricate decorations ornamented the walls and roofs of the minute chapel and of the twin pavilions on either side of the main building that housed the kitchens and the staff.

Inside the château, which was divided into two small suites, the rooms were walled with colored porcelain tiles or lined with Chinese brocade. In each suite there was an aviary filled with exotic birds whose cheerful chirruping filled the air and provided a charming accompaniment for the lovers in the blue and white Chambre des Amours.

It was the garden, however, that was the most enchanting of the delights of the Trianon de Porcelaine. Designed by Lenôtre and brought into existence by hundreds of workmen under the direction of the king's head gardener at Trianon, Le Bouteux, the garden was approached from the canal by a double staircase leading up onto a parterre lined with orange

Versailles under construction looked more like a pathetic ruin than the grand château it was to become. In this painting multitudes of workmen swarm over the rubble-strewn meadows and the half-completed stables (right), some of them hoisting timbers, some cutting stones, some mortaring, measuring, and giving directions. Undaunted by all the hubbub, the king arrives in his carriage at the château's main gate (center, rear), while in the foreground his chief minister, Jean Baptiste Colbert, looks over the architect's plans.

Whole armies of gardeners were kept busy tending Versailles' vast expanses of trees, shrubs, and flowers, ripping up old displays and planting new ones sometimes as often as twice and three times a day in order to satisfy the king's whims. The woodcuts reproduced here depict men at work amid an array of boxed trees in the orangery (near right) and laying out the design for a garden (far right).

trees and filled with such quantities and varieties of flowers that visitors were overwhelmed by the sight and the smell of them. So overcome by the dense, exotic smell were the visitors one hot sultry day, in fact, that they were obliged to retreat from the garden to seek less headily perfumed air. On other, less unfortunate occasions visitors, having passed through masses of varicolored blooms, through banks of wallflowers, jonquils, hyacinths, and jasmines, on their way in to supper, were amazed as they passed out into the gardens again after the meal to find that — by some apparent miracle in defiance of nature — the beds and borders were now filled with masses of entirely different flowers. Even in the middle of winter flowers set in pots were made to appear as if they grew in the soil of the gardens at the Trianon de Porcelaine and were sometimes changed for other flowers not once but twice a day. To achieve this extraordinary metamorphosis, Le Bouteux was supplied with nearly 2,000,000 flowerpots so that his men could take all kinds and numbers of flowers from his hothouses at any season of the year they were required and place them in the beds at the Trianon.

Intended as a private retreat, the Trianon de Porcelaine thus soon became a showplace—although Louis and Athénaïs de Montespan did manage to spend hours by themselves there, sitting on the moss-covered seats in the secret bowers of the parterre, making love in the great bed in the Chambre des Amours.

The Trianon de Porcelaine, however, was not the monument to the king's love for her that Mme. de Montespan really desired. She hoped for something altogether more imposing, a château that might even rival Versailles itself. When she was shown plans of a fine house Louis offered to build for her outside Saint-Germain, she turned them down with scorn. They might do very well for some actress, she commented haughtily; they would scarcely do for her. So the king gave her the Château de Clagny.

Louis first thought of building a fine house at Clagny for Athénaïs in 1674, and soon there were twelve hundred workmen there. The architect was not Le Vau's successor, Dorbay, who had completed the Trianon de Porcelaine, but a young protégé of Colbert, Jules Hardouin-Mansart.

To many it seemed a curious choice, for few people had ever heard of Mansart who was then only twenty-eight years old. In a few years, however, his reputation stood higher than that of any other architect in France, and he was appointed first architect to the king. He owed this sudden fame and fortune to his designs for Clagny.

The ground plan of the house was simple and conventional enough. As with Le Roy's first small château at Versailles, this new structure was to be built around three sides of a courtyard, the entrance front facing east, the garden front west. The central block was to consist of state apartments, each room opening into the next by means of doorways so aligned that the whole length of the building could be seen from end to end. The south block was to contain the great gallery, extending along the south garden front and having a series of small rooms behind overlooking the courtyard. The north block was also to contain a series of cabinets overlooking the courtyard, and on the north garden side a long suite of reception rooms. Projecting

to north and south on each side of the central block were to be single story wings, the one on the north containing further cabinets and offices, the one on the south an orangery which could be entered either from the garden or from the great gallery. The long façades of each of the three main blocks were to be broken by three slightly projecting pavilions.

Once work was begun, Louis and Athénaïs were equally anxious to see it finished. When he was away at the wars, the king wrote constantly to Colbert to ask for reports of its progress, while the marquise drove over three or four times a week to supervise the building in her commanding way, to discuss new ideas and possible improvements, to insist upon alterations both in the details of Mansart's design and in Lenôtre's plans for the gardens.

The gardens at Clagny were, she insisted, to be as remarkable as those at the Trianon de Porcelaine; and so they turned out to be, although Lenôtre, who did not share the king's passion for flowers, was able to give them a less exotic appearance. He was allowed to preserve a small wood, and the lake, whose waters stretched far away into the distance, seemed perfectly natural. The big orchard of orange trees was artificial, of course; but the tubs in which the trees stood were hidden behind palisades covered with tuberoses, jasmines, and carnations. The Marquise de Sévigné thought it all "beautiful, surprising, enchanting."

No one loved it more than Mme. de Montespan herself, and she longed for the day when she and her children could be established in comfort there. She was an extremely fertile woman; she already had two children by the king and expected to have, as she

eventually did have, several more. For the moment, however, the arrangements that had been made for her existing children seemed perfectly satisfactory to her. They were being very well looked after by her friend Mme. Scarron.

Françoise Scarron was the granddaughter of Théodore Agrippa d'Aubigné, a Huguenot soldier and historian, one of Henry IV's most intimate friends, and the daughter of Théodore's son, a wild reprobate who had murdered his unfaithful wife. Imprisoned for a subsequent crime, the younger Théodore had married the prison governor's daughter. Françoise was their third child. She was brought up first by severely Protestant relatives of her father, then by devotedly Catholic relatives of her mother. After long and determined instruction by the Ursuline nuns in Paris, she became a Catholic herself. The next year, Françoise married Paul Scarron, a poor, gnarled, and paralyzed poet old enough to be her father.

There could be no physical love between Scarron and his young wife, but they were deeply attached to each other. When her husband died eight years after their marriage, giving her permission to remarry in his will — since he himself had "forced her to fast and that should have given her a good appetite" — Mme. Scarron chose not to do so. She determined to remain in mourning and entered a convent as a lay boarder; she spent most of her time helping her friends when they needed her. A devout woman, she was also extremely good-looking. She was clever and witty, too, and that was what appealed to her friend, the Marquise de Montespan. But she was sometimes caustic and often disapproving. And conversations with her frequently

The sumptuously decorated staircase at left, with its crystal chandelier, its gilded emblems and borders, its polished marble and trompe l'oeil mural, was the entrance to the queen's apartments. After her death in 1683 King Louis took up residence in this wing and the staircase became the main entrance to the royal chambers. At right, in a group portrait after the original by Pierre Mignard, the king's second great love, the fertile Mme. de Montespan, is surrounded by her offspring, the royal bastards.

turned upon matters of religion and problems of moral behavior. Men did not immediately warm to her.

The king certainly did not. He liked clever, amusing people, as he told his sister-in-law, but he did not like the kind of carping, intellectual woman that he supposed Mme. Scarron to be. And when his mistress suggested her name as a suitable person to be entrusted with their children, he did not take at all kindly to the suggestion. Nor did Mme. Scarron. She had no wish to be involved with some shifty arrangements for royal bastards. But the king was persuaded; he would find it difficult to place his children in better hands. Françoise Scarron was reliable, discreet, of good family (on her father's side), and she was fond of children. And Mme. Scarron was persuaded; the position that was offered her would bring money, security, and no doubt eventually rank. She began to waver but would make no firm decision until she had spoken to her confessor. The confessor said she must certainly have nothing to do with the upbringing of a baby born of her friend's adulterous relationship with an unknown father; yet if the king admitted that he was the father and asked her to become responsible for the child, the priest advised, she would have to accede to his request.

A house was thereupon bought in a Parisian suburb, and servants were engaged to run it. The first baby — a girl who soon died — was carried there secretly one night by Mme. Scarron. Within the year a baby boy, who was to become the Duc de Maine, a pretty, precocious, clever child, was brought there too. The king, noticing how upset Mme. Scarron was by the death of his baby daughter — much more upset than the mother was — and noticing, also, how well she was bringing up

his promising little son, began to like Mme. Scarron rather better than before. She, for her part, began what she later described as the long struggle for the king's soul. The Marquise de Montespan, assured and proud and voluptuous as ever, for the moment felt no concern.

As yet neither the building of the Château de Clagny nor the advent of Mme. Scarron into the lives of the king and the Marquise de Montespan had had any effect on life at court. But in the year that Clagny was begun the enlarged château at Versailles was at last rendered suitable for prolonged visits by the king, who had previously gone there only for short periods and usually in connection with some *divertissement* held on the grounds. After 1674, however, Versailles became the main haunt of the court.

The king himself had apartments on the first floor in the central block with west windows facing the gardens and south windows looking down upon the marble flagstones and the fountain of the Cour de Marbre — into which no one except princes and dukes, marshals of France, and ambassadors was permitted to enter without special permission. Next door to the king's rooms were those of the Marquise de Montespan, whose south windows also looked down upon the Cour de Marbre; and men took pains to avoid walking beneath them when it was supposed that she and her lover were together — to do so was known as walking before the firing squad.

The queen, whom no one had cause to fear, also lived on the first floor in rooms that faced across the southern parterres and the orangery toward the Pièce d'Eau des Suisses. They were approached by the queen's staircase, a beautiful creation in which the

ghosts of Louis XIV's Versailles still seem to linger.

Louis XIV, however, had not yet finished with his
château. He had succeeded in transforming his father's
maison de plaisance into something more like a palace,
but to him it still appeared to lack a certain essential
grandeur. He had few criticisms of the noble west
front, which Le Vau had designed for him, but he
thought that the contrasting styles in the east entrance
front should in some way be unified into a more
splendid whole. He called in the young Mansart, who
had succeeded so well at Clagny, to advise him.

Soon Versailles was once again covered with scaffolding: smiths and plumbers, stonemasons and marbleworkers, joiners and glaziers appeared in their thousands — at one time more than 35,000 men and 6,000
horses were at work on the buildings and in the
gardens.

Colbert, growing old and ill, and burdened with
many other duties, strove as best he could to supervise
the work and administer its finances with his accustomed efficiency. Finding it all too much for him, he
enlisted the help of his son, the Marquis d'Ormoy, for
whom he obtained the appointment of Superintendent
of Buildings, but the son was not the man his father
was. "If you want to succeed," Colbert told the young
man, "you will have to get up every morning between
five and six, go straight to visit all the workshops, see
that the masters of the works are there, count the number of workers and check that they are right; put aside
two hours for this visit, listen to all the workmen, find
out what they need, see that they get it immediately;
then go to your office and do two or three hours work
revising all the memoranda of what is to be done, give

the orders for everything, inspect, verify, check the
prices. After luncheon you must make another visit,
see the works, again count the workmen. . . ." But such
industry and method, practiced throughout his life by
the father, were beyond the capacity of the son; and the
king upbraided Colbert, who had so strongly advised
him against building at Versailles at all, both for the
cost of the work and for its slowness. The Minister of
War, the Marquis de Louvois, Louis added reproachfully, did not find it necessary to spend nearly as much
on his military fortifications.

The malicious comment went all the deeper to the
old man's heart for he hated and distrusted his un-
scrupulous rival, who he knew was only too anxious
to supplant him. Indeed, Louvois did supplant him.
Worn out by the wear and worry of his ceaseless yet
thankless work, Colbert fell ill and died in 1683, before Mansart's new designs had been carried into effect
— and the aggressive, deceitful Minister of War came
to Versailles to take his place.

Although repeatedly complaining to Colbert about
the rising expenses of the work at Versailles, the king
had decided, long before it was finished, to build yet
another château in the park in which he could entertain a select circle of his chosen friends. The Trianon
de Porcelaine was too small for this; the Château de
Clagny belonged to the Marquise de Montespan. So
he built Marly.

He had chosen the site, as his father had the site for
Versailles, while out hunting. It was an open, marshy
place, surrounded by woodland and commanding a
lovely view toward the Seine. The château itself was
built on rising ground facing south toward the river;

in front of it the land fell away in terraces enclosed by neat rows of trees and ornamented by a series of artificial lakes. On either side of the lakes was a row of evenly spaced, identical pavilions, six on each side, joined one to the other by lines of pergolas. The twelve pavilions were each divided into two small apartments, one above the other, connected by an oval staircase, paneled and furnished in crimson satin, and provided with all that a guest would need, even to a nightshirt and a hairbrush. There were an additional twelve apartments in the château, four of them permanently reserved for members of the royal family. Only a fraction of the court, therefore, could be entertained at Marly at any one time and invitations there — a mark of the king's high favor — were eagerly sought and had to be solicited. "Sire, Marly?" became a question that was asked at Versailles with the most tense expectancy.

As they caught their first glimpse of Marly over the banked-up terrace that concealed it from view of the vulgar, guests fortunate enough to receive invitations to the new château were immediately struck by the extraordinarily beautiful colors of the place. The brightly gilded balustrades and window frames of the château and the surrounding buildings, the painted statues in the gardens, the colored pictures of the birds and animals and flowers that decorated the glistening fountains seemed framed by nature's deep and varied greens in summer and golden browns in autumn. Due to the *trompe l'oeil* skill of Jacques Rousseau and other painters employed at Marly, every façade appeared to be adorned with busts, with gold and blue bas-reliefs, and by red marble pilasters.

The guests were received in the huge octagonal salon, a magnificent — if, in winter, cold and drafty — room that occupied most of the inner core of the château; the private apartments, each decorated and furnished in a different color, were arranged around it. It was a confusing as well as a splendid room, for in each of the four walls that did not contain windows that looked into the radiating vestibules there was an identical mirrored door; and after a few turns around the floor beneath the four *oeil-de-boeuf* windows of the high dome, it must have been difficult to remember how to reach the gardens again.

Most guests, indeed, were happier in the gardens, which were enchanting. There were secluded arbors with little seats where they could talk, intrigue, or watch the fountains playing and the waters of the lakes rippling in the sunlight. There were artfully contrived walks in the woods leading to cascades and to open spaces where they could play pall-mall — a game in which the object was to drive a wooden ball, with a mallet, through a suspended iron ring. There were paths leading down to a wrought-iron balustrade at the gardens' southern end where stood the twin horses designed and executed by Antoine Coysevox, and beyond these horses, in the distance, could be seen the roofs of Saint-Germain.

Those privileged friends invited to the king's parties in the gardens at Marly became aware before the house was finished that Louis was growing tired of the Marquise de Montespan as he had grown tired of Louise de La Vallière. He spent less and less of his time with her; he even seemed to avoid her.

At first no importance was attached to the hours he spent talking to Mme. Scarron. She was an attractive

woman, to be sure, with a handsome figure and lovely brown eyes, but it was difficult to imagine her, three years older than the king, in the role of his mistress; it was supposed that she was helping him write his memoirs. The plain black clothes she always wore, her devoutness, her rigorous sense of duty, her rather managing efficiency all seemed more suited to the schoolroom than to the boudoir; and she was, indeed, proving herself an excellent governess to the king's illegitimate children by the Marquise de Montespan. The eldest of these, the Duc de Maine, had grown into a delightful child, intelligent, bright, lively, and good-looking — so much more appealing than the dull, fat dauphin who was nine years his senior though with but a fraction of his self-confidence.

It was not the dauphin's fault that at seventeen he was awkward, shy, and wholly uninterested in learning; for he had been most cruelly brought up by a tutor and a governor, both of whom had beaten him savagely in an effort to knock his lessons into his head. The Duc de Maine, on the other hand, was being educated by Mme. Scarron with care and patience; and the king, remarking the contrast between the two boys, gave due credit to the younger one's governess. She was, he discovered on better acquaintance with her, not nearly so tiresome and forbidding as he had at first supposed. She had high intelligence as well as high ideals; conversations with her were a great deal more satisfying than the flippant exchanges of gossip and banter he had grown accustomed to with Mme. de Montespan.

Athénaïs began to feel vaguely concerned. Her friend, she knew, was not in the least likely to go to bed with the king, but these long conversations about morals and religion were on no account to be encouraged. She decided it was time that Mme. Scarron was discharged from court. She found a duke willing to marry her; but Mme. Scarron was quite content to remain a virgin and a widow. Athénaïs next found a famous nunnery in need of a new abbess; but Mme. Scarron was quite content to remain in the outside world. And the king, while agreeing that the governess should be generously rewarded for her excellent services, was also averse to her departure from the court. He gave her the money to buy a moated château between Rambouillet and Chartres. Its name was Maintenon. Its new owner, the governess Mme. Scarron, became the Marquise de Maintenon — and the court at Versailles began to take more notice of her, to whisper and to wonder. "I do not know which forked tongue among the courtiers first pronounced the new name," Mme. de Sévigné told her daughter, "but in any case they are calling Mme. de Maintenon *Mme. de Maintenant* under their breaths. . . . This *dame* de Maintenon or de Maintenant passes every evening between eight and ten o'clock with His Majesty. M. de Chamarande escorts her there and brings her back quite openly."

III

The Seat of Government

On Easter Sunday 1675 the king astonished Versailles by paying devout attention to those religious duties that he had performed in former years with a perfunctory indifference. He went to Communion, he confessed, he sent the Marquise de Montespan to Clagny. Later in the year, when he rode off to the wars again, he did not even trouble to say good-bye to Athénaïs. It seemed, unlikely as it was, that Mme. de Maintenon's warnings about the consequences of continuing to lead so unvirtuous a life at last had had their desired effect.

On Louis's return from the front, however, he gave orders for the Marquise de Montespan's apartments at Versailles to be prepared for her once more and immediately upon his arrival he headed straight for his mistress's bedroom. It appeared that the affair would go on as before; and for a time it did. But there were those at court who said that this was only because Françoise was away from Versailles, having taken the Duc de Maine to a spa to seek a cure for the boy's half-paralyzed leg. They were right. No sooner had she returned than there were quarrels and distressing scenes, particularly over the children whom their mother indulged by giving them sweets between meals and allowing them to stay up late. Mme. de Maintenon, furious at this breach of the strict rules she had laid down for the children's conduct, complained to the king. And the king, who knew how conscientiously she looked after the children when they were ill and when their mother was gambling, and whose taste for order and regularity was as deep-seated as that of their governess, took her part and blamed his mistress.

He was nevertheless displeased with both of them for creating such tedious and ill-mannered disturbances, and he escaped from their company into the beds of less demanding and less tiresome women. He began an affair with the beautiful, red-haired, and mercifully placid Princesse de Soubise which lasted, in an intermittent way, until she contracted scrofula and lost a front tooth. Simultaneously he made advances to Mlle. de Ludres, a pretty, haughty maid of honor who — so Mme. de Montespan darkly warned him — had "scurf all over her body." Occasionally he made love to Mlle. des Oeillets, an actress's daughter who was Mme. de Montespan's maid, and to the Marquise de Thianges, Mme. de Montespan's sister. And then, in 1678, he gave Athénaïs still further provocation by going to bed with Mlle. Marie Angélique de Fontanges, a deliciously attractive girl of eighteen, "beautiful as an angel and stupid as a donkey."

The king, fascinated by her at first sight, had Marie Angélique installed in a little bedroom near his own so he could spend the nights with her, but he ignored her during the day lest Mme. de Montespan should make a scene or Mme. de Maintenon give him a lecture. But Mlle. de Fontanges was not a girl with whom a man could hope to share a secret; nor was Versailles a place where any secret could easily be kept. Soon this latest affair was the talk of the palace. In her triumph Mlle. de Fontanges drove around the grounds in a pearl-gray carriage drawn by eight horses and appeared at mass wearing a dress of the same material as her lover's coat and wearing the same pale blue ribbon as his Order of the Holy Spirit.

Abandoning all restraint in his infatuation with this sensuous, silly girl, Louis walked with her and rode

with her constantly, as though he could not bear to leave her side. And to Mme. de Montespan's fury and Mme. de Maintenon's disgust, he made the stupid little creature a duchess with a yearly allowance of 20,000 écus. The affair, however, died as quickly as it had begun. In December 1679, the newly created duchess gave birth to a baby boy who died the following month, and immediately upon her return to court she herself fell seriously ill. Her body began to swell, her beautiful face became puffy, she cried continually. The doctors cupped her but could not stop the bleeding; and the king, overcoming his distaste for the sickroom, went to visit her — and left weeping to see her so changed. She rallied a little, then relapsed, recovered for a time, then grew worse. Mlle. de Fontanges died on June 28, 1681. The Duchesse d'Orléans was not the only person to believe she had been poisoned, but the king advised the Duc de Noailles, her sole companion when she died, "as regards the question of having the body opened up, I think it would be better if that could be avoided."

There had been more than enough scandal at court already. In January of the previous year six of its most fashionable yet least respectable denizens had been arrested on charges of poisoning, and in the lengthy trials that followed many terrible charges had been made.

It appeared that numerous courtiers from Versailles were in the habit of visiting Paris for the purpose of calling upon one Catherine Monvoisin, known as La Voisin, a fortune-teller of wholesome, indeed kindly appearance whose wide range of lovers included a count and an executioner. She was indeed a versatile woman. As well as telling fortunes, she arranged for abortions and black masses, dealt in aphrodisiacs and poisons, and had a limitless stock of cures for all manner of physical defects and emotional misfortunes. One of her most regular customers, so her daughter said, was none other than the Marquise de Montespan.

Years before, it was alleged, Mme. de Montespan had enlisted La Voisin's help to make the king fall in love with her, to harm all other rivals for his affections, and to render the queen sterile. Later she had used La Voisin's potions against both Louise de La Vallière and Mlle. de Fontanges; she had impregnated her rivals' clothes with arsenic and red sulfur; she had allowed an accomplice of La Voisin, an ancient, derelict abbé, to celebrate mass on her behalf over a woman's naked body — probably her own — with the blood from the cut throat of a stillborn baby and to make up the baby's heart and entrails into a magic potion. In desperation she had even tried to kill the king when the love philters she administered to rekindle his passion for her did nothing more than give him headaches and make him tired.

The king refused to believe all this. Perhaps Mme. de Montespan *had* tried to cast a few spells, *had* slipped an aphrodisiac now and again into his drink, but both he and Mme. de Maintenon refused to believe that she had attempted poisoning. And when the body of Mlle. de Fontanges was cut open, in defiance of the king's wishes, it was found that her stomach and intestines were quite healthy: the young woman had died of pneumonia.

Mme. de Montespan — despite all the suspicion that surrounded her — was kept on at court, was appointed

The view from Louis XIV's bedroom window, which is reproduced in the 1690 painting at left, below, reveals the perfect symmetry of Versailles' design. The forecourts, with their confusion of courtiers, sedan chairs, horsemen, and parading troops, open out majestically to the rolling hills, while the receding line of the wings is gracefully completed by the twin arcs of the stables. Masterpieces in their own right, these equine palaces housed all the king's horses and all the king's pages as well, and here the sons of the nobility also received an education. A section of one of the stables is shown in the photograph at left, while the close-up at right gives a detailed view of the three surging horses that crown the central arch.

Intendant of the Queen's Household to soften her fury at the honors bestowed upon the stupid Fontanges, and was granted a present of 17,000 *écus*. But the affair between Athénaïs and Louis was definitely over. After the birth of her last baby, the Comte de Toulouse, Mme. de Montespan grew fat and ungainly; her thighs became a most unprepossessing size; she drenched herself in so much scent that the king felt quite ill in her presence; and above all, she was alternately so savagely ill-tempered or so affectedly gay that it was no longer any pleasure to be in her company. The king sought it no more. He seemed far more interested in the new buildings at Versailles which were almost finished.

On May 6, 1682, the king officially announced that henceforth Versailles was to be the seat of the French government. And although the scaffolding, the cranes, and the winches had not yet been removed, the debris, wood shavings, and stone chippings had not yet been carted off, and thousands of men and horses were still at work in the gardens, he arrived to take up residence as if making a triumphal entry. Later that year Mansart's work was completed at last, and a new, more magnificent Versailles was revealed.

It was seen, on the entrance front, that the whole château had been provided with that new style of handsome curb roof each face of which had two slopes, the lower one steeper than the upper, known by the name of its original designer, Mansart's great-uncle, François. It was also seen that the two pairs of square buildings housing the offices that Le Vau had built on the northern and southern extremities of the front had been amalgamated into two long wings to provide larger and more imposing offices as well as accommoda-

tion for the officials of the government. To the east of these, their sweeping concave fronts facing onto the Place d'Armes, were the two magnificent stabling blocks — one for the coach horses, the other for the riding horses — that led the Elector of Hanover to protest that the King of France's horses were better housed than he was himself at home in Germany.

On walking around the sides of the new château, the curious visitor would notice with pleasure the skill with which Mansart had broken the monotony of the immensely long façades by punctuating them with colonnades and statues and rows of urns and trophies along the tops of the parapets. And, on coming around to the western front, he would be delighted by the transformation that the young architect had worked. For here a splendid new gallery had been built along the entire recessed front, and Le Vau's windows had been raised and arched so as to complement the new proportions.

This new gallery, the Grande Galerie — or Galerie des Glaces as it came to be called — was one of the wonders of Versailles. Under the direction of Charles Le Brun, scores of painters, as well as sculptors and plasterers, glaziers, metalworkers, and marbleworkers had spent month upon month to make this chamber the most magnificent and glittering reception room in Europe. It was, in fact, as the Marquise de Sévigné decided when she first saw it, "unique in the world." Lighted by crystal chandeliers of an enormous size and intricate workmanship and by hundreds of smaller candelabra, the gallery was lined with solid silver console tables, *guéridons,* and flower tubs of exquisite workmanship. The highly polished parquet floor was cov-

ered with Savonnerie carpets; the ceiling was vividly painted with allegorical figures; the whole length of the inside wall was hung with huge looking glasses in which were reflected the tall arched windows overlooking the garden; and in alcoves between each set of three windows were large marble statues of perfect grace.

In the new château, the life of the court began quite early. Unless he had specified some other time the night before, the king was awakened at eight o'clock by his First Valet of the Bedchamber, who slept in the room with him on a truckle outside the gilded balustrade that surrounded the royal bed. When he was awake, his First Physician and First Surgeon entered the room, shortly followed by his former wet nurse who kissed him on the cheek. Since he usually sweated a great deal in the night and was scrupulously clean — he changed his linen three times every day — Louis always had his whole body well rubbed down with spirits before the arrival at a quarter past eight of the Great Chamberlain, who ceremonially reopened the curtains around the bed which the masseurs had left closed. The Great Chamberlain offered His Majesty holy water from a basin at the foot of the bed; this was a sign that any courtier who had the privilege of the *grande entrée* — that is, the right to accompany the Chamberlain into the room — might now approach the bed to speak to the king or ask him a favor.

The Great Chamberlain then handed the Book of the Office of the Holy Ghost to the king who said the Office while the Great Chamberlain and the rest of the company retired to the adjoining anteroom. When he had finished, risen from his bed, and put on his slip-

pers, dressing gown, and wig, Louis summoned the company back into the room. He then gave permission for those who had the lesser privilege of the *second entrée* to be admitted and, after them, the more inferior members of the court. While the latter were arriving, he began to dress, taking off his dressing gown, putting on his undergarments, stockings, knee breeches, garters, and shoes — then getting back into his dressing gown. It was all done with "consummate grace."

Every other day the king was shaved, keeping on his wig, talking to those around him about some inconsequential affair such as hunting or gardening, and watching the barber's progress in a looking glass held for him by a servant. The shaving completed, he knelt down beside his bed to say his prayers; the clergy present in the room knelt with the king but the courtiers remained standing.

He then sat down to a light breakfast of bread and wine, before completing the *Grand Lever,* which was performed to a strict routine — each particular article of clothing was handed to him by a privileged member of his family, a court official, or a servant. The First Valet of the Bedchamber, for instance, helped him put on the right sleeve of his shirt, but the First Valet of the Wardrobe helped him put on his left sleeve. A *Cravatier* arranged the neckcloth, but the Master of the Wardrobe put it on. Once the *cordon bleu* had been placed over his shoulder, his coat upon his back, and he had been handed and taken, one by one, his hat, his gloves, his lace handkerchief, and his cane, the *Grand Lever* was over.

It was then time for the morning's business with his ministers, for interviews, and for issuing orders for the

day's work. Mass was celebrated in the chapel at half past twelve; the congregation stood with their backs to the altar facing the king, who knelt down on a velvet cushion in the royal tribune — a procedure, as one observer said, that seemed "to indicate a sort of subordination, for the people appear to adore the king and only the king to adore God." After mass there was a council meeting every day except Thursday, which was reserved for private audiences, and Friday, when the king made his confession. If there was time before dinner at two o'clock, he then usually called upon his current mistress.

Since the main meal of the day was not served until the evening, the midday repast was either *au petit couvert* or *au très petit couvert*. But the king had a voracious appetite, so even if the lighter *couvert* had been ordered it would always prove to be a substantial meal of at least three courses, each made up of several different dishes. The king ate alone, various attendants standing by his chair. Often his brother was there to hand him his napkin, and if Monsieur remained standing for some time after the napkin had been graciously accepted, the king would ask him if he wished to be seated. The following courtesies would then be observed: Monsieur would bow in acquiescence, the king would order a chair, and after a few minutes would say, "Brother, pray be seated." Monsieur would bow again and sit down. He would remain seated until the meal was over, when he would stand up to take back the king's napkin. Sometimes, if he had come over especially from his château at Saint-Cloud, Monsieur would be invited to share the meal — but this privilege was rarely accorded him. No women were ever present,

except occasionally the queen and the Maréchale de La Mothe, who had retained the privilege from the days when she used to be the royal governess.

After the meal the king would spend a short time playing with his beloved dogs and giving them biscuits. Then he would take some form of exercise, either walking in the gardens, shooting, or hunting. There were six packs of hounds in the kennels, five hundred pairs in all; and stags, boars, and wolves all abounded in the royal forest. Louis would go out in all weathers, apparently unaffected by heat or cold and caring little about rain. He needed fresh air, otherwise he suffered from headaches, an ailment that he attributed to having spent so much of his early life with his nostrils filled with the smell of heavy scent. For years, one of his courtiers said, he had not cared for any perfumes stronger than orange water, "and anyone who approached him had to be very careful about this."

When Louis strolled around the gardens, any courtiers were free to follow him, but they were not permitted to wear a hat, for this was a privilege reserved for promenaders at Marly, where the king might suddenly say, "Gentlemen, your hats!" At this they would all put them on, and woe betide anyone who did so clumsily.

On his return from his outing he would sometimes spend an hour or so in the Turkish bath in the Appartement des Bains on the ground floor of the château and then settle down to further work before the main meal of the day. This was usually served about ten o'clock, though frequently the king was tardy, and the royal family had to wait impatiently for him, sometimes until as late as half past eleven.

Supper for the king was a huge meal. Observers were

astonished by the amount of food he consumed; Mme. de Maintenon said, with more than a hint of disapproval, that if she ate half as much she would be dead within a week. He would begin with four big platefuls of different thick soups, each of them, like every other dish, previously having been tasted as a safeguard against poisoning, and one of them often being *Soupe Colbert* which contained poached eggs — he loved eggs and would eat them boiled one after the other. After the soups the king would quickly but elegantly consume a whole bird — partridge, chicken, or duck — stuffed with truffles, a big dish of salad, followed by mutton well flavored with garlic, and two thick slices of ham. These courses were usually followed by pastry, preserves, and crystallized fruit. All would be eaten with knives and fingers, for forks had not yet come into fashion. The wine was usually a still, light champagne — a bubbly champagne had been invented in 1670 by Pierre Perignon, the cellarer of the Abbey of Hartvilliers, who used a cork instead of a wooden stopper, but this was as yet not much favored — or Burgundy mixed with water.

It was as well that the king enjoyed cold food, for the route to his table from the kitchens beyond the southern block of the château was an extremely long one. Guarded by various attendants and three armed soldiers, the procession of dishes had to be carried across the rue de la Surintendance, into the south block, up a staircase, along various corridors, vestibules, and salons, through the Grand Hall of the Guards, into the upper vestibule of the marble staircase, and across the Hall of the King's Guards. Any courtier who happened to meet it during its lengthy progress through the château had to salute the royal meal by sweeping off his hat, bowing, and uttering, in a reverential voice, the formula, "the king's meat."

After the meal there was generally some sort of entertainment, a ball or a concert or, in summer, a trip down the canal in a gondola. And there was nearly always gambling. Indeed, Versailles was often known as the *tripot*, the gambling den. The card games were very simple, luck counting for much more than skill, and the amounts lost and won were enormous. The king himself liked to play for high stakes, and occasionally he enjoyed a game of *brelan* or *reversi*. But he much preferred billiards, which he played in the Salle de Diane while listening to his orchestra playing in the Grande Appartement.

These evening pleasures were far from universally enjoyed. "Everything is more stiff, more reserved, more constrained and also less free than is typical of the nation's general character," noted one courtier. "Even the entertainments seem to lack spontaneity and appear stiff and formal, with a sense of constraint reigning over the pleasures."

According to the Duchesse d'Orléans:

The *appartement* is an absolutely intolerable experience. We all troop into the billiard room and . . . squat, no one uttering a word, until the king has finished his game. Then we all get up and go to the music room where someone is singing an aria from some old opera which we have heard a hundred times already. After that we go to the ball. Those who, like me, do not dance have to sit there for hours without budging for an instant, and can neither see nor hear anything other than an interminable minuet. At a quarter to

ten we all follow one another in a quadrille, like
children reciting the catechism.

At the gambling tables, however, all restraint was
thrown away. "The players behave like madmen," the
duchess went on, "one screaming aloud, another striking the table so hard with his fist that the whole room
echoes with the sound, a third uttering blasphemous
oaths so terrible as to make one's hair stand on end;
they all appear to be completely out of their minds."

When it was time to retire for the night, the king
proceeded to his bedroom for the ritual of the *Grand
Coucher,* as elaborately choreographed a ceremony as
was the *Grand Lever.* After each garment had been removed and handed to the appropriate attendant with
customary and practiced grace and the king was in his
night attire, he bowed to the company who thereupon
backed out of the room leaving the king alone with his
servants and those few courtiers privileged enough to
watch the *Petit Coucher,* a short ceremony during
which His Majesty's hair was combed and brushed. To
hold the candle at the *Petit Coucher* was one of the
highest honors to which a courtier at Versailles could
aspire, and one which many a nobleman endured
months of boredom and discomfort to achieve.

For all its occasional delights, life at Versailles was
rarely either pleasurable or comfortable — though always expensive. The king insisted on every courtier being well dressed on all occasions; frequently a death, a
birthday, or a marriage in his family would prompt
him to order everyone to wear new clothes. This, for
the men, entailed new long, brocaded coats and embroidered waistcoats, new ribbons for their shoulders,
new silk bows for their necks, new high-heeled, square-

57

*To the enlightened seventeenth-century mind
formal gardens like those at Versailles (below) —
hedged, trimmed, and carefully laid out in precise
geometrical patterns — represented the triumph
of man over nature, of civilization over barbarism.
A carelessly meandering branch or twig or blade
of grass was immediately seized upon and snipped,
clipped, pressed, or mowed back into its assigned
place. A rigorous formality was also practiced in
Louis's court, where none but the king could don
a hat unless the king himself gave his permission.
Thus, in a detail from the painting at right a
nattily hatted Louis is shown being wheeled about
his gardens accompanied by a few friends — all
of them respectfully bareheaded.*

toed shoes, new ostrich plumes for their hats, and very likely new full-bottomed wigs. The ladies also had to provide themselves with new silk, or brocade, embroidered dresses, new ribbons, and new satin shoes. The expense for some was ruinous and often led to a plea, to the king or one of his mistresses, for a sinecure, which would enable the insolvent courtier to pay off his debts, or for permission to leave Versailles for a time and make an effort at retrenchment upon some distant country estate.

The king, however, was reluctant to allow anyone to leave Versailles for long. He liked to keep his nobility under constant observation, to observe their behavior and their temperament, to judge for himself their suitability as officers in the army and as trusted servants of the state. So Versailles, as Bishop Bossuet said, was more than a palace, it was a town. Up to five thousand people lived there in the winter, their daily routines organized with almost as much strictness and regularity as the army officers among them would be forced to grow accustomed to when the summer campaigns began.

In the daytime, when these thousands of people were at large in the gardens, the corridors, and the courts, when sedan-chair men were pushing their way through the throng, and servants were rushing about upon their masters' errands, it was scarcely possible to imagine where they could all sleep at night. And, indeed, many of them slept in the tiniest and gloomiest of garrets. The long wing that enclosed Le Vau's *enveloppe* to the north, the Nobles' Wing, was a warren of little rooms and cabinets, corridors and cupboards. Many of the rooms had small windows that opened upon blank walls, never upon the sky, let alone upon the sun, and some garrets had no windows at all. The more pleasant apartments were occupied by richer families, such as the Noailles, who had a whole series of apartments leading off a long corridor known as the rue de Noailles. But even these richer families, whenever they could, went away to spend the night in the far more pleasant atmosphere of their houses in the town of Versailles. Naturally, with so much overcrowding, the château itself was rather a dirty place — though far less so than the doge's palace at Venice, where the very stairs, as Baron von Archenholz complained, were like a sink. There were privies in the courtyards at Versailles, but a night commode was an essential piece of furniture in every apartment.

The most commodious apartments at Versailles, other than the royal family's, were those opposite the Nobles' Wing, where the king's acknowledged illegitimate children and their households lived. In 1682 there were eight of these children; four others had died in infancy. The two eldest were Louise de La Vallière's children: Marie Anne, who was sixteen, and Louis, Comte de Vermandois, who was fifteen and had only one year left to live. Mme. de Montespan's surviving children, apart from the Duc de Maine, then aged twelve, were Louis César, Comte de Vexin, who was to die in 1683 at the age of eleven; Louise Françoise, then nine, who was to marry Louis de Bourbon-Condé; Françoise Marie, aged five, who was to marry Monsieur's son the Duc de Chartres; and Louis Alexandre, Comte de Toulouse, a child of four.

The king's only surviving legitimate child, Louis le Grand Dauphin, known at court as Monseigneur, was

then twenty-one. He bore little resemblance to his father in either appearance or manner — he was large and fair, shy and rather clumsy. His passion for hunting was as obsessive as that of his grandfather; he had his own pack of hounds and took them out every day after mass. He also had a deep love of works of art, pictures, porcelain, and fine furniture; and his rooms at Versailles, as light, as spacious, and as elegantly decorated as any in the château, were filled with his treasures.

Monseigneur was a most good-natured fellow, and when the king suggested that he should marry, he readily agreed and even showed no alarm or reluctance when the princess chosen for him was Marie Anne Christine Victoire of Bavaria. He might well have been excused some qualms, for this daughter of the Elector of Bavaria turned out to be, in a courtier's unkind words, "not just ugly but so grotesque that Sanguin, the king's chief maître d'hôtel, who had been sent by the king to Bavaria during the negotiations for the marriage, felt compelled to warn His Majesty on his return: 'Sire, do not betray your emotions when you see her for the first time.' " Her lips were said to be very pale, while her hands were very red; her nose was broad and her forehead was covered with brown marks; her teeth looked uniform but most of them were rotten. The king, concerned to let so ill-favored a young lady loose upon the gossip of the beauties of Versailles and wondering, no doubt, what sort of grandson might be produced from such a stock, thought it would be better if the marriage negotiations were brought to an end. But the dauphin, on the contrary, was quite ready to go ahead. He did not mind ugly women, and at least this one was said to be otherwise presentable and

she spoke good French. So Marie Anne came to France; Monseigneur married her without demur; and she was soon pregnant.

The baby was born at Versailles, on a suffocatingly hot August morning, soon after the government's transfer to the palace in 1682. It was an appallingly difficult birth, and it was feared that the mother might die. The king spent much of his time in her room, hoping that his presence might give her courage, being kind and considerate to her, offering her wine and food. The dauphin, who had grown quite fond of his wife, now suffering so acutely, sat crouched miserably in a chair, surrounded by all the muttering, jostling spectators who had the right to attend a royal birth.

At last the baby was born and the king announced in a clear voice, "We have got a Duc de Bourgogne!" According to the Abbé de Choisy this announcement "brought wild enthusiasm."

All those present permitted themselves the liberty of embracing the king. The crowd swept him along with them. . . . He allowed himself to be embraced by anyone who wished. The common people seemed to have taken leave of their senses. Bonfires were lit everywhere in celebration of the event. Some chairmen were so bold as to break up their mistress's gilded sedan-chair and burn it in the courtyard of the Galerie des Princes, adding to the blazing heap some pieces of panelling and flooring that were stacked there waiting to be installed in the gallery. Bontemps [the king's chief *valet de chambre*] came running to the king in a rage to tell him of this vandalism; but the king simply laughed and said "Let them be, we can soon order new floorboards."

To ensure her recovery the doctors wrapped the dauphine in the skin of a sheep that had been flayed alive in her room, while her husband — knowing that he could do nothing to help her and that the king would not require him at his council — went out hunting as usual.

The king never did require either his son or his brother at his council. Indeed, he treated them both with a kind of affectionate contempt. "Now we are going to work," he would say to Monsieur. "Go away and amuse yourself, *mon frère*." And Monsieur, a dark, neat, extravagantly dressed little figure, would mince away obediently. It distressed the king deeply that his brother was so ineluctably and obviously a homosexual, for he himself detested the homosexuality that was rife at Versailles.

The curé of Versailles, François Hebert, was most eager that the king "should act firmly to put an end to these detestable vices," and he enlisted the help of the virtuous Mme. de Maintenon, asking her to use her influence to suppress "such fearful corruption." Mme. de Maintenon replied that she had tackled the king about the problem on several occasions, but he had replied with resignation and sadness, "Am I then to begin with my own brother?"

Nevertheless, in June 1682 a great number of distinguished courtiers, accused of "ultramontane debaucheries," were exiled from Versailles. The king had gained the evidence upon which they had been dismissed from his fifteen-year-old son by Louise de La Vallière, the Comte de Vermandois, who was deeply involved. Upon being questioned sternly by his father, he broke down and confessed everything. He was ex-iled to Normandy. Other exiles included the Prince de La Roche-sur-Yon, nephew of the Prince de Condé, the Prince de Turenne, the Marquis de Créquy, the chevaliers de Sainte-Maure and de Mailly, and the Comte de Roucy.

This purge did not, however, rid Versailles of homosexual practices. The Comte de Bussy, Mme. de Sévigné's cousin, wrote:

Debauch reigned more supremely here than anywhere else in the world. The complaisance with which all the ladies offered themselves rendered their charms so unattractive to the more youthful courtiers that hardly any of the young men even glanced at them any longer . . . and although the king expressed on several occasions his absolute horror of these kinds of pleasure, it was the one manner in which he could never gain obedience. Wine-bibbing and the unmentionable vice were so fashionable that there remained very few who preferred to pass their time in a more agreeable manner.

One day, the count said, the Duc de La Ferté, the Comte de Berain, and Colbert's son, "all dead drunk, sent out for ice-creams and, finding that the vendor was a well-made young boy, wanted nothing better than to use him as a whore. When he struggled to defend himself, they struck him twice with the flat of a sword."

The personable Italian Primi Visconti was himself approached by the Marquis de La Vallière, brother of the king's former mistress. "Monsieur, in Spain, the monks," the marquis suggested; "in France, the nobility; in Italy, everyone. . . ." Visconti retreated hastily, and protested that he was "very far from such thoughts," that he was twenty-five and had a beard. Vallière answered that "for Frenchmen of good taste

The marriage of the Grand Dauphin and his wife proved fertile, giving Louis XIV three grandsons, who are shown on the opposite page in a family portrait done in 1687 by Pierre Mignard. The eldest, Louis, the Duc de Bourgogne, is standing (right); Philippe, the Duc d'Anjou and the future Philip V of Spain, is seated with a dog on his lap; and the youngest, Charles, Duc de Berry, is seated beside his mother. The boy Louis would have succeeded the dauphin as king, but Louis XIV outlived them both. The king's brother (left), the Duc d'Orléans, known as Monsieur, also proved a potent element in the family genealogy, despite his penchant for boys. He fathered eleven legitimate children by his two wives, the second of whom, Elisabeth Charlotte of Bavaria, is shown in the portrait below, and his descendants filled all the Catholic thrones of Europe.

neither age nor growth of hair was a consideration. . . ."

Monsieur's two favorite catamites were the Chevalier de Lorraine and the Marquis d'Effiat. The chevalier, "looking like the painting of an angel, placed himself entirely at Monsieur's disposal," the Abbé de Choisy said, "dispensing favors and giving orders in so lordly and authoritative a manner that he might have been taken for the master of the house." Monsieur appeared to be completely dominated by him, and his wife, Henrietta Anne, hated him for it. When Henrietta lay dying, she felt convinced that she had been poisoned; after her death it was widely believed that the Chevalier de Lorraine and the Marquis d'Effiat had been jointly responsible. But although there were many suspicious circumstances, the doctors could find no poison in her body, and after a period of disgrace, the Duc d'Orléans's two friends were readmitted to the court at Versailles.

Soon after their return, Monsieur married again. His second wife was Princess Elisabeth Charlotte of Bavaria, a big, outspoken, masculine, fair-haired woman, known at the French court as Liselotte. What little time there remained to her when she was not out hunting, she spent writing long, indiscreet letters to her German relations whose portraits covered the walls of her room.

Monsieur feared that he would never be able to make love to such a massive, robust woman. He succeeded well enough, however, and before they decided to sleep in separate rooms, he had provided himself with three more children. One of them, Philippe, was to become regent upon the king's death and great-great-grandfather of the last of the kings of France.

IV
Decline of the Sun King

The larger his family grew, the more Louis XIV felt the need of a house where he could live with his relatives from time to time free from the restrictions and necessary routine of the château's daily life. Casting his eye across the park of Versailles, he considered various sites before deciding that there was only one that would serve his purpose well: he would build a new house where stood the Trianon de Porcelaine. Devised in the days when he was so much in love with the Marquise de Montespan, the extravagantly decorated little blue and white pavilion was no longer to his taste — nor did memories of the happy times he had spent there accord well with thoughts of the blowsy, quarrelsome woman that his former mistress had by then become.

The king therefore determined to pull the building down and to erect in its place a more solid house worthy of his family and of the new style of life that the Marquise de Maintenon had so successfully encouraged him to adopt. Instead of the elaborate ornamentation and fanciful *trompe l'oeil* effects of the Trianon de Porcelaine, he would have real and substantial plaques, columns, pilasters, and carvings; this was not to be a painted bauble but a piece of sound, imposing architecture. In 1687 Mansart and Robert de Cotte were set to work and soon the Trianon de Marbre was rising to take the place of the Trianon de Porcelaine.

Louis took as much interest in the building of his new château as he had taken in the construction of Versailles itself. Frequently he would come to inspect the work in progress, and once detected an irregularity in one of the windows — an irregularity so slight that no one else had noticed it. Indeed the Marquis de Louvois, who had taken over responsibility for the

king's buildings since the death of Colbert, refused to recognize any lack of uniformity. The king insisted that the line was out of true; measurements were accordingly taken and his sharp eye was proved correct.

When the pale yellow stone and pink marble château was finished, invitations to stay there were as eagerly sought after as they were to Marly. In fact, an invitation to the Trianon de Marbre was deemed an even greater honor than permission to attend the king at Marly. A lady invited to stay at Marly was allowed to assume that she might bring her husband with her. But if she were invited to the Trianon de Marbre a separate application had to be made in order for her husband to be of the party. And by refusing the application, the king could — and often did — demonstrate his distaste for an undesirable courtier.

One of the most charming features of the Trianon de Marbre, as it had been of the Trianon de Porcelaine, was the garden. Although much of the original garden was retained, less emphasis was now placed upon neat flower beds and parterres, more upon shady walks, trees, and grass and, above all, water. Indeed, at every turn guests strolling in the gardens would come upon stone and gilded fountains tinkling sprays of water into shell-shaped basins.

Here at the Trianon de Marbre, as in the gardens of the château at Versailles, the king had insisted upon a fine display of fountains. As Lenôtre well understood, a garden laid out symmetrically in regular, balanced, complementary shapes requires the play of water; otherwise the effect is one of dullness rather than of harmony. But the problem at Versailles was that the existing supply of water was never quite ade-

quate to the heavy demands that were made upon it.

There were no fewer than 1,400 fountains on the grounds and to keep them constantly in play as the king liked to see them was a task beyond the capacity of the most expert engineers. It was found impossible to keep all the fountains going at once for any longer than three hours at a time and then only during fetes or upon the occasions of visits by distinguished guests from abroad. Usually just the fountains nearest the château were kept playing and these were turned off at night. As additional fountains were placed in the gardens at the king's request, it became impossible to supply them all with water at the same time; and it required the utmost ingenuity to ensure that when His Majesty took a walk around the gardens each fountain came into play as soon as he came within sight of it and was turned off so as to conserve the water supply immediately after he had turned his back upon it. This necessarily frequent manipulation of the taps and the difficulties of maintaining the requisite pressure led to repeated breakdowns that were sure to arouse the king's irritation. Evidently little trouble was experienced with the fountain in the Cour des Marbres which was kept in play all day and night, but the sprays of other fountains in the gardens were much given to dwindling to dribbles at the most inopportune moments. "You must arrange for the pumps at Versailles to work properly," the king instructed his Superintendent of Buildings after a maddening succession of failures. "When I come back I want to find them in a condition that will not exasperate me by their breaking down all the time."

All manner of devices were employed to improve the water supply. Windmills and horses laboriously pumped water from the lake at Clagny; other mills pumped away in secluded places at Versailles. But the supply was never sufficient, and stagnant water rendered the air at Versailles a considerable danger to health. One hot August almost everyone at Versailles apart from the king himself was taken ill on account of the foulness of the air.

On the king's orders, ever more expensive and wasteful projects were undertaken. Consideration was even given to an attempt to divert the waters of the river Loire to Versailles — until it was realized that the scheme would entail the improbable discovery of a method of making the stream thus created flow uphill. Then a more realistic plan was suggested by which water could be drained from the plateau beyond Saint-Cyr by means of a complicated system of underground conduits, syphons, aqueducts, reservoirs, and canals. Work began and was continued at enormous cost of both money and lives. Workmen were lost by the score, killed by the natural hazards of the enterprise which, at the king's order, was carried out at a furious pace and — so it was alleged at the time — by the poisonous fumes given off by the opening up of so much unwholesome earth. The number of deaths among the laborers was "prodigious," according to Mme. de Sévigné, who alleged that every night one could see bodies being carted away for secret burial.

The king, however, paid no regard to the loss of life. Workmen, like soldiers, were expendable. He had no understanding of ordinary people nor sympathy for them in the hardships of their lives. Mme. de Maintenon said that it was no earthly use speaking to him about the miserable conditions in which most of his

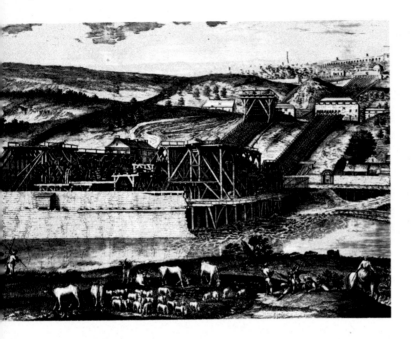

people lived; it merely made him cross. Constantly urged to alleviate the deplorable lot of prisoners in the country's terrible prisons, he did nothing. And once when a woman insulted him in a public place, he had her soundly whipped even though it was explained to him that her mind had gone after the loss of a son killed in an accident during the building of Versailles.

If Louis ever considered the workmen who perished in bringing water to Versailles he did not show it. Water he wanted; water he would have. While canals and reservoirs were being constructed as far from Versailles as Rambouillet and Epernon, appeals were made throughout the country for people to give advice as to how other sources could be tapped. A landowner, who had installed a huge pump on his estate at Modaves, proposed the building of an even more enormous pump to bring the waters of the Seine into the high ground north of Versailles beyond Rocquencourt.

A model of the proposed machine was made and proved successful, so work began. By means of 14 immense water wheels and 221 pumps the water was carried up the slope from the Seine Valley to the hills of Louveciennes where an aqueduct was to be built to take the waters down to the gardens of Versailles, Marly, and the Trianon de Marbre. Even this great undertaking failed to provide all the water that was needed, and recourse was then had to the building of another and even longer aqueduct to bring down to Versailles the waters of the Eure.

The task of building this aqueduct was entrusted to Marshal Vauban, France's greatest engineer, whose military fortifications were one of the marvels of the age. He was allowed 30,000 soldiers for the project,

which by the spring of 1686 had cost over 8,000,000 livres. The work, however, was then suddenly stopped. In May the troops working on it were required at the front at Neustadt and they never returned to Versailles. For by the end of 1688 France was once again involved in a costly war. On the death of the childless elector, the king had put forward a claim to The Palatinate, upon the frail grounds that the elector's sister, Liselotte, was now Monsieur's wife. And thus the aqueduct, almost complete when work on it was interrupted, was never finished.

These were sad days for France. The war was marked by none of the triumphs of earlier campaigns. Moreover, the revocation of the Edict of Nantes in 1685 was proving disastrous for France. By this edict, Louis's grandfather, Henry IV, had guaranteed freedom of conscience to French Protestants; revocation meant that many thousands of the country's most skilled and industrious citizens went abroad rather than submit to the detested Roman Catholic Church. Thus, in his efforts to create a united state, King Louis ruinously weakened it.

The Huguenots took their skills and industry to France's enemies and spread anti-French propaganda far and wide in Germany, Holland, and, above all, in England. Then, in 1688, William of Orange, the king's most implacable and most gifted enemy, took over the English throne in a bloodless coup against Louis's cousin, the Roman Catholic James II. King James fled for safety to the French court, and his successor as King of England, William III, prosecuted with ever greater determination the war of the Grand Alliance against France — a war that was to end with the Treaty of Rys-

wick in 1697 and the loss of many territories won in the years of Louis XIV's golden triumphs.

The misfortunes of France during these waning years of the seventeenth century were reflected in the gloom that settled over the court at Versailles. The queen was dead; and no one missed her very much. At news of her approaching death the king, in tears, had been seen running through the Galerie des Glaces to fetch the viaticum from the chapel. But he had recovered from his grief as quickly as he recovered from his sorrow at the death of his mother, and within two years, in the small oratory in his apartments, he had married the Marquise de Maintenon.

The ceremony was conducted in the utmost secrecy, for Mme. de Maintenon's humble birth scarcely marked her as a suitable wife for a king of France. But Louis was fond of her; at the age of fifty she was not likely to complicate the succession to the throne by having children, and, in any case, he had no need of additional heirs. His son, Monseigneur, was healthy enough and his daughter-in-law was evidently capable of bearing healthy children — the Duc de Bourgogne was followed by the Duc d'Anjou in 1683 and by the Duc de Berry in 1686.

Mme. de Maintenon was still good-looking; she was still amusing and witty yet discreet; she was deeply religious; and, above all, the king loved her in his way. "He loved me, it is true," she said after his death, "even if only as much as he was capable of loving." Certainly he enjoyed her company and spent more time alone with her than he had ever spent with anyone before. Naturally she made many enemies, notably Liselotte, the caustic Duchesse d'Orléans, who scarcely ever mentioned her without using some such epithet as "that old trollop," "hag," or "manure heap."

The king's new wife was widely blamed for the increasing dullness of the court at Versailles, since although she was witty she was not in the least high-spirited; she was worldly but she hated the life the court led; she continued to wear the dark clothes she had always worn and condemned the dissipations and frivolity of those more gaily dressed with acidulous disdain. "I am filled with horror at the very sight of Versailles," she protested. "That is what is called the world; that is where all passions are at work: love of money, ambition, envy, dissipation. How happy are those who have put the world behind them!"

Under her influence, new rules governing the pleasures and duties of the court were made. Plays were banned during Lent; gambling was discouraged; regular attendance at mass was required and the whispering that had previously been tolerated in chapel was now severely frowned upon. The young courtiers found the new regime intolerable and complained of it bitterly in their letters. The king's daughter by Louise de La Vallière, Marie Anne, who married Louis Armand de Bourbon, Prince de Conti, wrote of the boredom of life at Versailles and of being obliged to go out for long drives with Mme. de Maintenon. "Judge what fun this must be," she complained sadly. Her brother-in-law, François Louis de Bourbon, who succeeded Louis Armand as Prince de Conti — a brilliant, charming young man whom the king despised — was equally scathing, referring to the king as Monarch of the Stage and implying that the Stage was one upon which he, for one, would prefer not to be an actor. The

king was given the prince's letter, and grew to dislike the writer and his young friends more deeply than ever.

The king's ill temper was exacerbated by pain. For a long time now he had been suffering from an anal fistula upon which his doctors were reluctant to operate until they had tried out the surgery upon other, less important sufferers. According to the curé of Versailles, the Marquis de Louvois brought several of these sufferers to his house in the town to be operated upon there by the king's chief surgeon, Charles Tassy Félix. "Some died under surgery, and [Louvois] took the precaution to have them buried at daybreak, with no tolling of church bells, so that no one should know what was happening. But several patients were cured."

Encouraged by these successes, Félix pronounced himself ready to operate on the king; the time fixed for the operation was eight o'clock in the morning of November 18, 1686. The king showed no signs of fear or anxiety as he walked around the gardens of Versailles the day before; and he underwent the painful surgery with remarkable self-control. As the surgeon probed with a specially designed bistoury and cut and snipped with lancet and scissors, the king "bore it all," one of the assistant doctors reported, "with the greatest fortitude." All he said was, "Is it done, messieurs? Finish your work, and do not treat me like a king. I wish to recover as though I were a peasant."

From that same evening onward Louis received various official visits and held a council in his room as though nothing had happened. "One could see the pain written on his face," the Abbé de Choisy said. "His forehead was nearly always bathed in sweat from sheer faintness and yet he continued to give orders and in-

sisted that he be kept informed of events. He ate in bed, in public, and allowed himself to be seen twice a day even by the most minor courtiers." He was permitted nothing but soup, and although he was consequently always hungry, he grew increasingly better tempered and seemed quite cheerful. Sometimes he could even be heard singing to himself. A second and even more agonizing operation proved necessary in December. From this, however, he recovered permanently, and by the beginning of 1687 the king — now nearly fifty — was almost fully restored to health.

As the king's condition improved, the dauphine's declined. After the birth of her third son, the Duc de Berry, she was never well again. "Ah, my son," she said to the little boy, "how dearly your life has cost your mother!" She shut herself away in her room, suffering from deep, ineradicable depression. "The dauphine is most unhappy," Liselotte, who rather liked her and could speak German with her, reported in her characteristic way, "and although she does her best to please the king, the old hag [Mme. de Maintenon] sees to it that she is made thoroughly miserable every day. They force her to spend her life being bored. . . . Her M. le Dauphin cares about nothing in the world. He finds his pleasures where he can and is horribly debauched."

The king certainly displayed little sympathy for his daughter-in-law, and was as impatient with her as he usually was with invalids — ill though he had been himself. Her doctors said she was just imagining her ailments, and that was Louis's opinion, too. She could, of course, make her proper appearances at court if she wanted to. She, for her part, said that she would have to die to show that she was really ill. And when she

Another of Louis XIV's garden retreats, the
Trianon de Marbre (later called the Grand Trianon
to distinguish it from the eighteenth-century Petit
Trianon) is shown in these photographs. Built in a
corner of the park at Versailles, the château
combines classical proportions with fanciful colors.
Thus, the stately progression of arched windows
and Doric columns is brightened by pink marble,
checkered tiles, and gilded balustrades. As for the
gardens, guests entering through the forecourt (near
left) and passing through the peristyle (seen at far
left and in the background of the photograph
below) might be greeted by one set of blooms in
the morning and an entirely different array in the
afternoon. Sacked during the Revolution, the
Trianon was restored under Napoleon.

did die in 1690 and the doctors opened up her body
in the usual way, it was discovered that one of a multitude of disorders was gangrene of the stomach.

The dauphin, as Liselotte said, had already taken
to finding his pleasures elsewhere, though few others
than himself could suppose that they *were* pleasures —
since he seemed not to care about either the age or the
appearance of his women, often apparently taking a
perverse pleasure in selecting the most unprepossessing.

The Duc de Saint-Simon could not refrain in his
Memoirs "from giving a typical example of his fastidi-
ousness." On an agreed date a young actress whom the
dauphin had seen and admired at the Opéra was
brought to Versailles:

> She was with an unattractive older woman as chap-
> erone, and was shown into the anteroom of Monseig-
> neur's apartments. Advised that the women were
> there, Monseigneur opened the door and grabbed
> hold of the woman standing nearest to it, who, being
> the ugly chaperone, resisted vigorously. He, thinking
> she was being coy, pulled her in and locked the door.
> The other woman was highly amused by this error,
> and anticipated with pleasure her companion's dis-
> comfiture when she was ejected from the room and she
> herself was called in. Just then Du Mont [a co-director
> of the Opéra who served as the dauphin's *procureur*]
> entered the anteroom, was astonished to see her alone,
> and asked her what she was doing there and what had
> become of her friend. When she had told him, Du
> Mont rushed up to the door, crying, "That's not the
> one you want, you've taken the wrong woman!" No
> answer. Du Mont shouted and banged again, but still
> no reply. Finally, Monseigneur opened the door and

71

pushed the woman out. Du Mont presented the other, saying, "Wait, here she is." "No, the business is done," replied Monseigneur, "she will have to wait another occasion." And he closed the door again.

The dauphin's tastes being so well known, it came as no surprise to Versailles when, soon after his wife's death, he took as mistress the ugliest woman at court. This was Mlle. Emilie-Joly de Choin, one of the Princesse de Conti's maids of honor, the daughter of a governor of Bourg-en-Bresse, a member of the minor nobility. She was quite "remarkably ugly," Mme. de Caylus thought, "and possessed the kind of mind that shone in anteroom chatter, with her eternal recitation of everything she had just seen." Liselotte was, of course, even more scathing. To her Mlle. de Choin looked:

just like a pug-dog: she was low-built, with short legs, a round face, a snub nose, and a large mouth filled with rotting teeth, the stink from which could be smelled at the other end of the room. Her breasts were horribly overdeveloped, but Monseigneur was enchanted by this phenomenon and used to play on them like drums. . . . The dauphin accustomed himself to the smell of tobacco smoke so that he should no longer smell the vile odour of la Choin's rotting teeth.

Hideous as she evidently was, Mlle. de Choin was married secretly by the dauphin, as his father had married Mme. de Maintenon, but — unlike Mme. de Maintenon — she rarely appeared at court after her marriage. Indeed, few people willingly did so, for Versailles had become duller than ever. There were still games in the evenings, lotteries for little presents and desul-

tory rounds of cards; there were still occasional rides in gondolas down the canal; symphonies were still given in the Salle du Spectacle. But all the pleasure seemed to have gone out of the entertainments of the court. Jean de La Bruyère complained of the seriousness, the melancholy; and Mlle. de Lafayette lamented, "Always the same pleasures, always at the same hours, and always with the same people."

At Marly the king would occasionally try to enliven the proceedings by throwing bread pellets at the ladies during supper and allowing them to throw pellets back at him, and sometimes he would go so far as to throw not only bread pellets but apples and oranges as well. "On one such occasion, apparently," wrote the Duc de Luynes, "Mlle. de Viantais, maid of honor to the Princesse de Conti, was slightly hurt by the impact of some pieces of fruit thrown by the king, and she retorted by hurling at his head a whole dish of dressed salad."

Such rowdy games were no substitute, however, for the real pleasures that life at Versailles had once been able to afford, and the king seemed sadly aware of it. He "is letting himself go," Liselotte reported in the summer of 1694. "He is visibly sinking, and appears fat and old. He appears to have shrunk. His face has changed so that he is hardly recognizable; it becomes more lined from day to day."

Two years later the whole atmosphere of life was transformed by the arrival at Versailles of a bride for his eldest grandson, the fourteen-year-old Duc de Bourgogne.

She was a little girl of eleven, Marie Adélaïde, the daughter of the Duke of Savoy, who had married a

daughter of Monsieur and his first wife, Henrietta Anne. She was very short, with long, brown hair, wide-set brown eyes, full red lips and a pretty, clear complexion. "She was rather snub-nosed," the Marquis de Sourches noticed, "her forehead too wide and rather bulging, her mouth rather wide and full-lipped, attractive enough, though, except when she laughed and then she showed teeth which were too big and irregular. Her bosom seemed well developed for her age . . . but she was still a child, played with her dolls and joined in games of blind man's buff."

Although she was not very pretty, Marie Adélaïde completely captivated the king from the first. He went as far south as Montargis to meet her, and as soon as he saw her, he was delighted. Ignoring all her faults, except those crooked teeth and a very ill-contrived curtsy, he wrote Mme. de Maintenon that she was perfect, enchanting, all that he had hoped she would be, a little thin, perhaps, but that was her age; she really had a very pretty figure.

When the bride-to-be arrived in Versailles, Mme. de Maintenon was charmed by her, too. "We are all in transports of joy at the treasure we have received," she assured the child's mother.

She only has to speak to show her natural wit, and her manner of listening and all the motions of her face make it abundantly clear that nothing escapes her. Your Royal Highness can scarcely imagine how great is the King's satisfaction. . . . Yesterday when I tried to stop her caressing me because, as I said to her, I was too old, she replied: "Ah, you are not very old!" Then she pressed herself eagerly against my lap and said: "Mama has told me to express to you the great affec-

Princess Marie Adélaïde of Savoy, who appears on the previous page as the Duchesse de Bourgogne, was a child of twelve when she married the duke, himself only fourteen. The royal wedding, which took place at Versailles in 1697, is portrayed in the engraving below. In attendance are the young duke's grandfather, Louis XIV (left), and the bride's step-grandmother, the Duchesse d'Orléans (right). The engraving opposite depicts the baptism of the couple's firstborn in June 1704, with the duchess abed in the background and four generations of royalty in the foreground: the king (seated), the Grand Dauphin to his right, the Duc de Bourgogne to his left, and the duke's newborn son in swaddling clothes. The child, in direct line of succession to the throne, died within a few months.

tion she has for you, and to ask you for your own affection towards me; do teach me, I beg you, what I must do to please you." Those are just words, Madame, but the air of gaiety, gentleness and charm which accompanied them cannot be described.

The wedding took place on December 7, 1697, not long after Marie Adélaïde's twelfth birthday. That night the Ambassador of Savoy was called to her room so that he could report that he had seen her in bed with the Duc de Bourgogne. In accordance with the king's instructions, however, the bridegroom soon got out of bed and went into the room next door where he dressed again; then he went into his own apartments to sleep. After Christmas both bride and bridegroom were returned to the schoolroom.

The more he saw of the little duchess, the more deeply fond of her the king became. She was so lively, so affectionate, so refreshingly uninhibited. He went for long walks in the gardens with her; he took her for trips on the canal; he played with her. He could deny her nothing. She rampaged around his rooms, disordering all his papers — and he did not object; at mealtimes she jumped up and down in her chair, made tearful faces, sang songs, licked her fingers — and he merely smiled. She was given her own little theater, and the menagerie was enlarged to provide her with her own little house in the park.

In October 1699, when she was fourteen, the Baron de Breteuil, Master of Ceremonies, had the honor of bearing the candlestick as he conducted the Duc de Bourgogne to her bed. "The Duc left his room with a firm step and a joyful air," the baron said; and soon, so the Marquis de Dangeau noted in his journal, the

young man no longer wished to sleep by himself.

Thereafter, life at Versailles was as gay and exciting as it had ever been. There were constant fetes and balls and masquerades, repeated expeditions to Marly. For, as the Marquis de Dangeau told a friend, the king desired the Duchesse de Bourgogne to do exactly as she pleased and was sufficiently rewarded if she was happy. As though he wished the château to be worthy of the gay little angel who had rejuvenated life within its walls and had given him new *joie de vivre,* Louis began an extensive scheme of redecoration. New marble fireplaces appeared, new looking glasses, new ceilings; and in the gardens men were kept at work all through the night, planting woods and making paths, transforming whole parts of the grounds so that it seemed each morning, as Liselotte said, that fairies had been at work.

One of the little woods was named after the king's beloved granddaughter-in-law; other parts of the park were altered for her pleasure. Two courses were laid out for *mail,* a game rather like golf of which the duchess was very fond. A switchback railway, with a gilded chariot, was built for her on a steep slope on the southern boundary of the park. An elaborate swing was erected for her on the grounds at Marly. For the duchess, though her marriage had been consummated, was still a child — and the king still indulged her as a child.

Not everyone, of course, found Marie Adélaïde as appealing as did the king and Mme. de Maintenon. Many, indeed, condemned her as a spoiled, willful, flirtatious and irritating little brat. She was shrewd and spiteful, the Venetian ambassador concluded; although "quite servile" to Mme. de Maintenon, whom she called "Dear Mama," she absolutely loathed the Duch-

esse de Lude, her lady-in-waiting, whom she treated abominably, imitating and teasing her continuously. She also unmercifully teased and played practical jokes upon the huge, ungainly Princesse d'Harcourt: she placed fireworks under her chair and, on one bitter winter's night, she filled her bed with snowballs. She was equally rude to her aunts and, indeed, to most people of their generation, thinking nothing of ridiculing the appearance of the more ugly of them in a loud voice at the dinner table.

The Duchesse d'Orléans, Liselotte, considered Marie Adélaïde utterly undignified, writing — with the utmost distaste — of her rowdy games and practical jokes, her prancing about the gardens arm-in-arm with her ladies, her being dragged over the ground on her back by servants who held her ankles, her dressing up in fancy costumes. Once she persuaded the pretty Marquise de La Vrillière to lie in her bed — then, telling her grave and faithful husband that she was tired, she returned to her bedroom. The duke followed her, undressed, and jumped into bed beside the marquise, whereupon his wife appeared and, affecting the most violent anger, upbraided him for his perfidy.

This practical joke was harmless enough, but to those who disliked the Duchesse de Bourgogne no antics of hers seemed quite so typically tasteless as her behavior one evening before going to a play at Versailles. She was, recalled the Duc de Saint-Simon, "showing off her mastery of various languages" to the king and various members of the court when, upon the appearance of an old nurse, she went over to the fire, stood with her back to it, and, leaning forward over a fire screen, she held up the skirts of her bejewelled

court dress. The nurse, with one hand in her pocket, slipped behind her.

The king asked what they were doing. The duchess "burst out laughing and said she was only doing what she usually did before a play, but the king persisted. Then she said: 'Must I really tell you, since you have not seen for yourself? The truth is that I am having an enema.' 'What?' said the king, roaring with laughter, 'are you seriously telling me that you are actually having an enema at this moment?' 'Indeed, I am,' she replied. The king found the whole thing extremely amusing."

There were many others who, finding the duchess far from amusing, blamed the king's indulgence toward her for the constantly deteriorating standards in the dignity of the court. Ladies began to smoke pipes and sniff snuff; gentlemen appeared at supper in their hunting boots; obscene stories and verses were bandied about; gambling, formerly discouraged in wartime, was played by the duchess and her friends for stakes almost as high as those wagered by Mme. de Montespan; horseplay took the place of wit; etiquette, so rigidly enforced in the past, was all but abandoned. The Duchesse d'Orléans, a most conscientious respecter of form despite her ribald letters and conversation, sadly complained that Versailles no longer bore "the slightest resemblance to a court."

As the standards and the fortunes of the court declined, so did those of France itself. The king's acceptance of the Spanish throne on behalf of his grandson, the Duc de Bourgogne's younger brother, the Duc d'Anjou — to whom King Charles II of Spain had willed it as a fellow-descendant of King Philip III —

had led to the War of the Spanish Succession in 1701. Most of Europe allied itself against France, and the Duke of Marlborough and Prince Eugène of Savoy inflicted defeat after defeat upon a weakened French army. Blenheim, Ramillies, Oudenarde, Malplaquet — the name of each battle was more bitter than the last to the old king, now past seventy, who worked for long hours, mostly in Mme. de Maintenon's room, endeavoring to avert the expected catastrophe, reading and answering reports, issuing instructions to his generals.

By the winter of 1709 France seemed *in extremis*. It was so cold that even the seas on the Atlantic shore were frozen hard; crops were ruined; animals died; people starved. There were riots in Paris and a mob of women marched on Versailles demanding bread; the king ordered the army to stop them and to force them back. Even at Versailles the privations were acute. Old people died of cold in their rooms; the king melted down his gold plate and his silver furniture to pay for the long war. In spite of the pleas of Mme. de Maintenon, however, he would not economize on the building of the new royal chapel; it was as if he feared to anger God, who already seemed to be looking upon him with a baleful eye.

Work on the chapel, abandoned during previous wars, had been started again in 1699 under the direction of Mansart and Robert de Cotte and, after Mansart's death in 1708, of de Cotte alone. Although many of their contemporaries disliked it — including the Duc de Saint-Simon, who condemned the taste of the king and both his architects out of hand, complaining that the roof of the "horrible excrescence" that rose above the roofs of the château gave it "the mournful appear-

ance of an enormous catafalque" — the chapel to modern eyes is a delight. The light, white stone, in contrast to the brown, streaked marble of the palace itself, gives it an appearance of wonderful freshness, calmness, and purity. The sculpture by a variety of hands is superb. Van Clève worked here and Magnier, Guillaume Coustou, Le Lorrain and Frémin; and when Antoine Coypel was painting the ceiling, the king came every day to watch him. On April 25, 1710, when the chapel was finished at last, the king came to listen to the choir sing in it and was enchanted by the effect; a fortnight later, after it had been dedicated by the Cardinal de Noailles, he attended his first mass there.

Louis appeared to derive more comfort from services in his new chapel than he had ever derived from his religious duties in the past — and certainly in these last years of his life he needed comfort. His brother, Monsieur, had suffered a stroke in 1701 after a violent quarrel with the king about his treatment of Monsieur's son the Duc de Chartres, whose talents were treated as slightingly as those of the even more gifted Prince de Conti; soon after this stroke, Monsieur had died. His wife, Liselotte, who had grown rather fondly disposed toward her husband in their old age, went through his papers, burning all the love letters he had received from his young men — and then she hurried to Mme. de Maintenon, the "old hag," to beg her to intercede with the king so that she would not be packed off to a convent but might instead be allowed to remain at Versailles. Mme. de Maintenon, though well aware what Liselotte had been writing about her for all these past years, kindly arranged for her to do so.

The king had scarcely grown accustomed to the death of his brother when his trusted old valet, Alexandre Bontemps, died; then the deposed English king, his cousin, James II, died at Saint-Germain; and his death was followed by that of the Marquise de Montespan. Not that the king cared much about this; so far as he was concerned, he told the Duchesse de Bourgogne, Athénaïs had been dead ever since she had left Versailles twenty years earlier. Nor did he display any emotion at the death of the forty-five-year-old Prince de Conti; and even when the dauphin fell fatally ill with smallpox in 1711, at the age of fifty, he showed little more emotion. He shook like a leaf, Mme. de Maintenon said, when he heard the news of his only legitimate son's death, but he remained dry-eyed.

When the Duchesse de Bourgogne, now the new dauphine, contracted measles the next year, however, it was a different matter. Louis was as devoted to her as ever, perhaps even more than ever; for since the death of her first child in 1704, Marie Adélaïde had grown less boisterous and irresponsible, quieter, more graceful. She stopped teasing her husband and became a loyal and loving wife, while he — now that his father was dead and he was heir to the throne — grew less shy and brusque, more relaxed and confident. The king, noting with pleasure the change in his grandson, took him into his confidence, admitted him to his councils, and began to feel at last that he had a worthy heir.

Now the adored dauphine had measles and was seriously ill. Many people had already died of the disease in Paris that summer of 1712, and the dauphine — after nine difficult pregnancies, six of which had ended in miscarriages — was not expected to recover. The weaker she grew, the more violent emetics the doctors gave

LE CONVOY, ET POMPE FUNEBRE DE LOUIS XIV. à S.ᵗ Denis le 9.ᵉ Septembre 1715

her, the more frequently she was bled from the foot. At first she could not believe that she was going to die, but within the week she became so terribly ill and suffered such racking pain that she realized she could not recover. "Good-bye, beautiful duchess," she said to the Duchesse de Noailles. "Today dauphine, tomorrow nothing."

The dauphin was overwhelmed with grief. The Duc de Saint-Simon who saw him two days later "was horrified at his appearance. His eyes were glazed and staring, almost wild; his face had changed and was covered with large blotches that were livid rather than inflamed." He seemed almost relieved when he knew that he, too, had measles, which was likely to prove fatal. "I die with joy," he murmured at the end, glad to have shared his wife's suffering and to be following her.

The elder of the former Duc de Bourgogne's two surviving sons was now dauphin. But when someone addressed him by the title the little boy — though he was only five years old — protested. "Don't," he said. "It's too sad." He, too, contracted measles; and he, too, died. So would his brother, Louis, have died, no doubt, had not his governess carried him away to her room — away from the doctors — pretending that there was nothing the matter with him, and kept him warm and undisturbed until he was better.

The court sank into gloom. The king, despite his defeats in the protracted War of the Spanish Succession, refused to surrender to the Allies, even when all seemed lost, and by the Treaty of Utrecht in 1713 he at least secured France's prewar frontiers. But the finances of the country were in ruins and there was scant pleasure to be derived from what little life there

remained to him. He still went out hunting, but with less evident enjoyment than formerly, his face expressionless so no one could tell what he was thinking. And in the evening, at Marly or Versailles, all joy had left the beautiful rooms where once he had known happiness. There were no parties now; the formal yet graceful ceremonies of the past were carried out, when performed at all, with perfunctory, mechanical indifference. "We have no more court here," Mme. de Maintenon reported bleakly. *"Tout est mort ici."*

At the beginning of August 1715 the king began to have pains in his legs. His doctors thought that it was some sort of neuralgia, but it was far worse than that: it was gangrene. Toward the end of the month Saint-Simon saw him having supper in the presence of the court for the last time. He could swallow nothing but liquids and it irritated him to be looked at. Requesting the courtiers to leave the room, Louis asked to be put to bed. He was obviously in the most frightful pain, but he did not complain. It had never been his habit to make a fuss. He lingered on for days, suffering patiently, until one evening he could bear it all no more, and he pathetically asked Mme. de Maintenon if there were anyone in the room apart from herself because he thought he was going to cry.

The end came on the first day of September. The doctors had long since given up hope, and the prayers for the dying were being recited. Louis repeated the responses so loudly that his voice could be heard above those of all the priests and the murmurs of the people crowding around his bed, watching him die as they had watched him live. Suddenly he spoke again: "Help, O God, help me quickly." They were his last words.

V

Louis XV le Bien-Aimé

As he lay dying, the old king had asked that his five-year-old great-grandson be brought to his bedside. "Mignon," Louis had said to him, "you are going to be a great king. Do not copy me in my love of building or my love of warfare. . . . Remember your duty and your obligations to God; see that your subjects honor Him. Take good advice and follow it, try to improve the lot of your people, as I, unfortunately, have never been able to do. . . . My dear child, I give you my blessing with all my heart."

Soon afterward Louis XIV died, and the Groom of the Chamber closed the eyes and mouth of the drawn and yellow face. His nephew the Duc d'Orléans — Monsieur's second son by Liselotte — was now the regent. He went out into the Grand Appartement to declare in a loud voice that King Louis XIV was no more; then the Duc de Bouillon, wearing a black feather in his hat, walked onto the balcony to announce to the crowds that had gathered below the windows of the royal apartments, "The King is dead!" He returned, exchanged the black feather for a white one, and intoned the corresponding formula: "Long live the King!"

The Royal Bodyguard, already booted and spurred in accordance with the late king's wishes, stood ready, waiting to escort the new Louis XV to Vincennes, where it had been ordered that he should remain until the palace at Versailles had been aired and cleaned. But the court did not return. The pleasure-loving regent preferred Paris and the excitement of the Palais-Royale; and so, for almost seven years Versailles was abandoned. Visitors came and wandered about its deserted rooms and courts; Peter the Great stayed in the Queen's Apartment, asked for the fountains to be played for him, and returned to Russia with ideas for such a palace of his own.

Meanwhile, the boy-king grew up to be an attractive child, well-behaved, intelligent and good-looking, shy and reserved without being awkward or aloof. An orphan without brothers or sisters, he was desperately lonely; and since he never had anyone in whom he could confide, he remained a retiring, reticent, even secretive person for the rest of his life. But his governess, the Duchesse de Ventadour, had loved him and had treated him with such kindness that he cried bitterly when he was taken from her to be given up to a tutor. And the regent also was kind and affectionate, allowing him to attend the meetings of the council holding his cat, reminding him always that he was the king and that his uncle's duty was merely to help him, to tell him what was happening, to advise him.

At last, in 1722, the regent's adviser, Cardinal Dubois, fearing that further dissipations in Paris would kill him, persuaded the regent to return to Versailles. The regent gave way; but the cardinal's advice had come too late. Within a few months of the court's return, the regent was dead. He was succeeded in his duties by the Duc de Bourbon, head of the Condé branch of the Bourbon family, age-old rivals of the Orléans branch. Rather than risk the possibility that the young king would die without an heir and the crown thus pass to the new Duc d'Orléans, who was next in line, the Duc de Bourbon decided that Louis must marry as soon as possible and sire an heir.

By the age of fifteen, Louis was considered quite ready for marriage. Although reserved and shy, he was strong and lusty as well — and he had already displayed

his impatience at having to wait until the five-year-old Spanish princess, who had been chosen as his bride, was old enough to go to bed with him. Fearing the consequences of waiting so long, the Duc de Bourbon ignored the pained protests of the Spanish ambassador, sent the little infanta back to Madrid, and looked about for a more nubile bride.

For want of a worthier, richer candidate, the duke's eye fell upon Maria Leszczynska, the only daughter of the exiled King Stanislas I of Poland who had lost his kingdom by sharing the confident belief of Charles XII that Sweden was a match for the Russia of Peter the Great. The choice seemed exceedingly odd to Frenchmen, for Maria was not merely poor, she was plain, she was dull, she was unaccomplished, and she was nearly eight years older than the king. She was, however, healthy and, it was hoped, fertile.

The hope was justified. Upon her arrival at Versailles, the king expressed himself delighted with her, made love to her — so it was said — seven times upon their wedding night, nine months after which she gave birth to the first of their ten children. But although the wife was dutiful and fecund and the husband fond and uxorious, it turned out to be an unsatisfactory marriage, for Queen Maria grew duller and stuffier with each succeeding pregnancy. She also grew less and less inclined to submit to her husband's exhausting demands upon her and began to invent excuses for not welcoming him to her bed.

Overcoming his natural reserve, the king then embarked upon a series of affairs with women of the court — beginning with a housemaid and progressing to the Comtesse de Mailly, one of the several daughters of the Marquise de Nesle, a lady-in-waiting to his wife. Tiring of the countess, he fell in love with her sister, the Marquise de Ventimile, who died giving birth to his baby. To comfort him in his grief the king returned to the bed of the Comtesse de Mailly which, however, he soon forsook for that of another sister, the prettier, though far less pleasant Duchesse de Châteauroux. The duchess was a bossy, grasping woman who prompted her devoted lover to send the Comtesse de Mailly from Versailles and to quarrel with the queen.

In 1744 the duchess's numerous enemies were given grounds for hope that they might be rid of her. The king, unable to follow his great-grandfather's deathbed advice to forgo the pleasures of warfare, had left for the front, taking his mistress with him. At Metz he fell so ill that his life was despaired of. Believing that the time had come for him to receive the Last Sacrament and to confess, he felt obliged to send the duchess away and to summon the queen to attend him in his last hours. The Bishop of Metz insisted that the confession should be a public one, and the king was in no state to oppose the humiliating ordeal. The confession was afterward printed and distributed throughout France by the Church.

Little harm to Louis's reputation, however, was done by the confession. He was a popular monarch, far better loved by his people than his predecessor had been in his last years. "How sweet it is to be loved," he is supposed to have said, "but what have I done to deserve it?" Upon his slow recovery, he began to be known throughout France as Louis le Bien-Aimé. Blame was attached to those who had broadcast his belated, humiliating submission to the Church, while the Duchesse

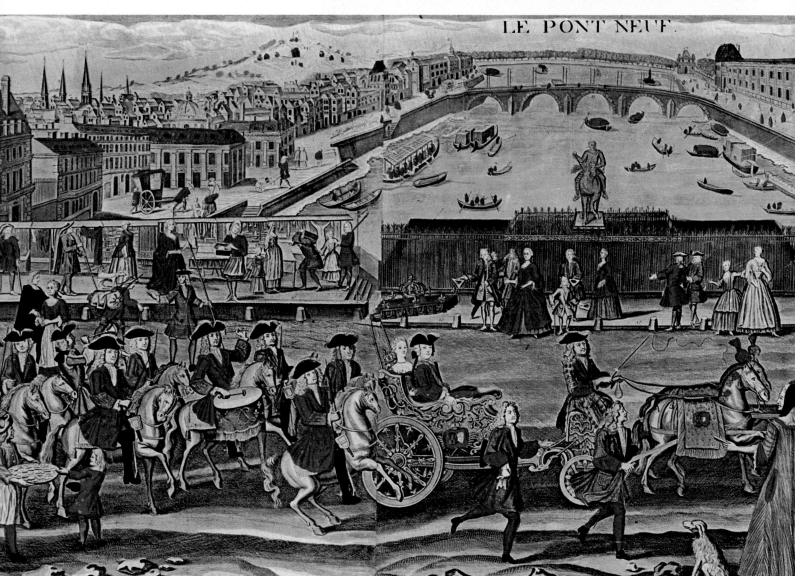

LE PONT NEUF.

de Châteauroux became more detested than ever. She
could not venture outside her house without being insulted and even molested by the mob; so distraught did
she become that she became ill and was forced to take
to her bed.

But the king could not do without her. As soon as
he got back to Versailles, he sent for her; and she,
anxious to resume her former dominant position there,
struggled out of bed, ill as she was, to obey his sum-
mons. She stepped into a hot bath, went outside, contracted pneumonia, and died. Louis, so recently saved
from the brink of death himself, withdrew into those
warrenlike recesses of the palace of Versailles that he
had constructed to escape from the prying attentions of
an inquisitive world.

The death of Louis XIV had not interfered with the
completion of the work at Versailles that had been
started late in his reign. The Salon d'Hercule, linking
the chapel to the Grand Appartement, was eventually
finished in 1736 to the designs of Mansart's pupil,
brother-in-law, and successor as First Architect, Robert
de Cotte. Its ceiling — a magnificent depiction of the
apotheosis of Hercules — was painted by François
Lemoyne. The fireplace is the only feature in this room
to suggest that it dates from the time of Louis XV and
not from that of his great-grandfather.

Elsewhere in the palace, however, the young king
had already begun to stamp Versailles with the taste
associated with his own strange personality. On the
upper floors, around the interior courtyards known as
the Cour des Cerfs and the Cour du Roi, he had built
a series of elegant little rooms joined together by miniature galleries and fanciful, winding, oval staircases.

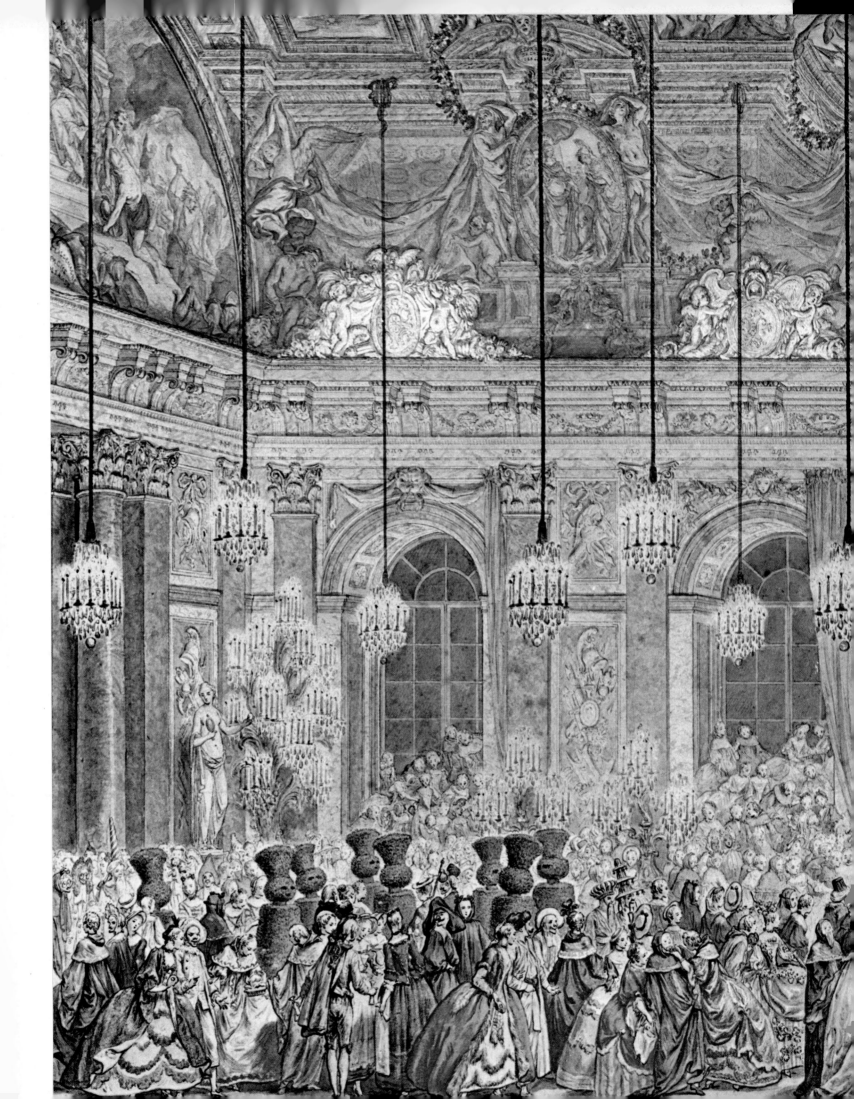

disguised as yew trees, their tops clipped in the shape of urns and holes cut for their eyes. No invitations had been issued, so for hours the concourses of carriages trundling up the Avenue de Paris to the Place d'Armes had been immense. The ushers, whose duty it was to require one member of each party to remove his mask and give his name at the top of the staircase, had had to abandon the attempt and to allow the heaving throng to push through the queen's rooms to the Galerie, to plunder the buffets of food and wine on the way.

The queen herself, not much given to this sort of frivolity, arrived unmasked; then came the dauphin, dressed as a gardener, accompanied by the new dauphine, a strange-looking woman with red hair, white eyelashes, and a huge nose, in the costume of a flower-seller. No one could recognize the king. One young lady, hopeful of succeeding the Duchesse de Château-roux as his mistress, was persuaded that he was one of the wobbling yew trees and excitedly left the Galerie des Glaces with him. But after she had gone, the real king removed his disguise and was seen talking in his attractive, husky voice to a vivacious girl in the fetching and appropriate costume of Diana, goddess of hunting. This was Jeanne Antoinette, Mme. Lenormand d'Étoiles. Reinette had come into her own.

Soon the king was in love with her. Tired, as he confessed, of going from one woman to another, he decided to establish her — bourgeois though her birth had been — as the *maîtresse en titre* at Versailles. First, however, it would be necessary to educate her in the ways and manners of the court, the numerous traditional regulations, the correct modes of address, the words that were used or were never to be used, how to sit down, how to rise when seated, how to cut meat with a knife, how to raise a wineglass to the lips, how to glide across the ground with fast and dainty steps as did the queens and concubines at the court in Peking of the Emperor Ch'ien Lung. Leaving her to her esoteric studies, the king went off to the wars — and to defeat the English at Fontenoy in May 1745 — and receiving good reports of her progress, he sent her the title deeds of an estate at Pompadour and made her a marquise.

The next step was to arrange for the presentation at court of the new Marquise de Pompadour, and this was a necessary formality to which he did not look forward with pleasure. However, soon after his return from the front, the Princesse de Conti was persuaded to present her and led her up to the Council Chamber where the king awaited her, his handsome features blushing scarlet as she entered the packed room. She curtsied three times in the approved manner, showing how well she had learned her lessons, and he nodded toward her dismissively, turning away in embarrassment. She was then taken to the queen whose reception of her — so much more gracious than she had expected — so overwhelmed her that she said far more in reply than etiquette required; and in removing a glove to take up and kiss the hem of the queen's skirt, she pulled off a bracelet which fell with a tinkle to the floor and which had to be retrieved by the Princesse de Conti.

Despite the hostility of the king's friend and his First Gentleman of the Bedchamber, the Duc de Richelieu, the Marquise de Pompadour was now accepted at court and immediately began to exercise over it an

Lovers and boon companions for twenty years, at last separated only by death, Louis XV and Mme. de Pompadour are portrayed here as they appeared shortly after their meeting at the Yew Tree Ball. The dashing portrait of the king, in armor and royal array, was done in 1748 by Maurice Quentin de La Tour, and is said to be an excellent likeness. Pompadour, depicted by court painter Jean Marc Nattier, is shown dressed in the alluring costume of Diana the Huntress, as she was at the ball where she snared her royal quarry.

authority that was to last for almost twenty years. Her benefactor, de Tournehem, became Superintendent of Buildings; her brother was created Marquis de Marigny; old M. Poisson was given a handsome estate, though he refused the title that was offered with it; and the marquise's former intellectual friends in Paris were benefited by her patronage, though she could not persuade the king — who did not feel at home in the company of writers — to invite them to his table.

Voltaire was commissioned to write an opera celebrating the victory of Fontenoy with King Louis portrayed as the Emperor Trajan. Later Voltaire came to live at Versailles in a room over the Prince de Conti's kitchen and was appointed King's Historian and Gentleman in Ordinary. Another of the marquise's intellectual friends, the writer Jean François Marmontel, was also found lodgings at court as well as a sinecure. A third contributor to the *Encyclopédie,* François Quesnay, joined his friends at Versailles and became the marquise's doctor.

Louis now spent nearly all his spare time with Mme. de Pompadour, going to her immediately after the conclusion of the ceremony of the *Lever* and staying with her until mass, returning to her after *déjeuner* on the days he was not out hunting, and remaining with her all afternoon until it was time to go to work with his ministers. Fortunately, the queen accepted her uncomplainingly and, indeed, grew fond of her, for the marquise behaved toward her in exactly the right way. The king showed his gratitude for his wife's toleration by treating her with much more kindness than he ever had in the past and by giving instructions for the queen's apartments at Versailles to be redecorated for

her as a surprise while she was away at Fontainebleau.

In Mme. de Pompadour's company the king was never attacked by those periods of intense boredom that had previously so often oppressed him; she knew just how to entertain him. She sang to him and played the clavichord for him, made him laugh with her funny stories and gossipy jokes; and although she was constitutionally and temperamentally unfitted to enjoy making love to him with his own persistent avidity, she never refused him as the queen had done. Above all, Mme. de Pompadour was able to retain the king's fascinated interest by being able to share with him so enthusiastically that passion for building against which Louis XIV had warned him on his deathbed.

When the Petits Cabinets at Versailles were finished, work began on the complete remodeling of the rooms formerly known as the Cabinets du Roi on the north side of the Cour de Marbre. This new suite of rooms, known as the Petits Appartements, was largely the creation of Verberckt and Rousseau. Decorated in white and gold, they were larger and grander than the Petits Cabinets above them, and the king, therefore, was able to entertain more people in them, sometimes inviting more than thirty guests to dinner.

The exquisite dining room in which these parties were held was made out of the bedroom and bathroom of Louis XIV's former suite, and was hung — like the other rooms in the Petits Appartements — with the king's most valuable paintings and fitted with his ever-increasing collection of *objets d'art.* In addition to the dining room, there was a bedroom, and next to this was the Cabinet de la Pendule — a room that took its name from an astronomical clock that gave the hour, the day, the month, and the year, as well as the phase of the moon. Above it was a crystal globe in which the planets performed their scheduled gyrations.

Beyond the Cabinet de la Pendule was the Cabinet Intérieur or Cabinet Intime where the king spent much of his time in the privacy in which he would have preferred to pass his whole life. The walls were covered with beautifully painted paneling, with carved wainscoting, with crimson and gold-braided damask hangings, with paintings by Holbein and Raphael. Next door to the Cabinet des Perruques was the Cabinet du Conseil, a room in which the crimson velvet of the king's sofa and the brocade of the armchairs and the folding stools, contrasting with the green velvet and gold-braided covering of the council table, was reflected in the tall looking glasses that lined the walls. Beneath the chimneypiece, in the middle of the hearth, was a cushion of the same crimson velvet as the king's sofa. On this sat the king's favorite cat, an enormously fat and prodigiously dignified white Angora. One day two of the king's attendants amused themselves by making this cat drunk on spirits of wine; the peals of laughter that greeted its consequent and highly uncharacteristic behavior brought the king into the room. Upon his sudden entrance, the attendants immediately stifled their laughter and, in answer to his question as to its cause, one of them said it was a story he had been relating. But then the king saw the cat lurching about the room. "Gentlemen, I will leave you now," he said reproachfully, "but if you wish to amuse yourselves, I ask you not to do so at the expense of my cat."

Mme. de Pompadour's apartments were those formerly occupied by the Duchesse de Châteauroux on the top floor, over the Grand Appartement, and thus most convenient of approach from the Petits Cabinets. Her rooms were crammed with furniture and pictures, with porcelain and all kinds of *objets d'art,* bibelots, and knickknacks. Approached by a lift that was made to move easily up and down by pulling on a cord attached to a counterpoise, these apartments commanded a fine view over the gardens of the palace, the Aile du Nord, and the Parterre du Nord. But fond as she was of her suite, Mme. de Pompadour was not content with so small a home for herself and her treasures. She induced her lover to build or buy all manner of other places for her, including the châteaux of La Muette, Saint-Hubert, Crécy-Couré, and Choisy, hunting boxes at Le Butard, Saclay, and Fausse Repose, and hermitages at Fontainebleau, Compiègne, and Versailles.

The Hermitage at Versailles was a charming, small one-story summer pavilion near the Bassin de Neptune, decorated inside like a farmhouse with simple painted furniture and cotton curtains. Its gardens were a delight; in variety and richness of color and of scent they rivaled those of Louis XIV's Trianon de Porcelaine; and as the Sun King's gardeners had done, so Mme. de Pompadour's renewed the flowers as often as her fancy dictated. One day there would be banks of oleanders and yellow jasmine, myrtle and tuberoses; the next, gardenias, lilacs, and roses would fill the bowers and trail beside the trellised palisades. Orange, lemon, and olive trees appeared to grow naturally on every side. The king loved animals, keeping pigeons, hens, and rabbits on the roof above his rooms in the palace; and his mistress, sharing this love, had a little farmyard at

Louis XV, more interested in matters of taste than in affairs of state, brought to Versailles a carefree gaiety that is reflected in the highly decorative if somewhat precious style of the period, such as the gilt trim of the marble mantelpiece above right. In the tapestry at left, The Hunts of Louis XV, *the craftsmen of the Gobelin factory not only rendered the details of trees and costumes with superb technical skill, they also gave the woven border the appearance of a gilt wood frame. Meantime, fine artistry and mechanical precision produced both the astronomical clock above, given to the king in 1753 and still in perfect working order, and the roll-top secrétaire at right, of inlaid wood decorated with bronze figures of Apollo and Calliope. With the turn of a key the top rolls up and all the drawers inside open simultaneously.*

the Hermitage. There were goats and cows, donkeys and hens; and it delighted Mme. de Pompadour to walk around the enclosure with the king collecting the eggs. Sometimes he would forgo a day's hunting to be alone with her at the Hermitage; and he would cook their meals himself.

After seven years of love there came a change in the relationship between the king and his mistress. She moved her apartments from the top to the bottom floor of the palace, an honor usually reserved for princes of the blood; she was created a duchess and in 1756 she became lady-in-waiting to the queen. It was understood at court that the thirty-five-year-old Mme. de Pompadour was no longer the king's mistress, but it was clear that his respect for her was unimpaired and that her influence over him was as strong as ever. The new apartments contained, as her former ones had, a private stairway to those of the king.

These new apartments, once occupied by the Marquise de Montespan, were previously known as the Appartements des Bains and contained an immense marble bath large enough for three people to use at the same time. This Mme. de Pompadour had removed and installed as a fountain in her garden at the Hermitage, and a more modern bathroom was built in the apartments in its place.

But Mme. de Pompadour was far from content with the mere installation of a bathroom; she gave orders for a wholesale remodeling which amounted to a complete reconstruction of this part of the palace. The cost, following so hard upon the expense of all the other works that had been carried out at Versailles and elsewhere to indulge the extravagant taste of the king

and his mistress, placed a great strain upon the resources of Lenormand de Tournehem's department. At one time the artists employed were "absolutely without funds."

Yet soon after Christmas the apartments were complete; Verberckt's beautifully carved paneling and Martin's paintwork were ready for Mme. de Pompadour's critical inspection, and she moved in. It was not, however, until the flooring had been taken up again and guncotton and flock had been stuffed between the joists to deaden the sounds from the State Apartments above, that she was entirely satisfied with the grand accommodation that she was to occupy for the rest of her life.

Once Mme. de Pompadour had settled comfortably into her new home, the king took a succession of mistresses one after the other — pretty working girls, actresses, prostitutes, who were either lodged in a small garret in the palace or in the Parc aux Cerfs, a villa in the town, until the king grew tired of them and moved on to the next. Many of them never knew who he was; they were told that he was a rich Polish relative of the queen who would reward them well for their services; and since the rewards were generous they professed themselves satisfied. The king made use of their services so often that his physician warned him of the dangers of such repeated lovemaking. Louis replied that he had been assured it would do him no harm provided he used no aphrodisiacs. "Ah, Sire," the doctor said, "change is the greatest aphrodisiac of all!"

But as long as the king changed his mistresses so often, Mme. de Pompadour could feel that her own position was as safe as ever. Once or twice her enemies

hoped that the king was falling in love and would replace her with a new *maîtresse en titre*. There was the gorgeous Louise O'Murphy, daughter of an Irish cobbler, who was François Boucher's favorite model and whose features were thus to be seen in many pictures at Versailles; and there was the Marquise de Coislin who shared the beauty and the charms of her cousins, the sisters de Nesle. But Mlle. O'Murphy fell from grace when she had the impertinence to ask the king, referring to Mme. de Pompadour, "What terms are you and the old lady on now?" And Mme. de Coislin followed her into oblivion when she asked for favors that could not be granted to anyone other than Mme. de Pompadour herself.

So Mme. de Pompadour continued to reign; and she and the king remained as happy together as ever, until one cold January night in 1757 when she heard dreadful news that she feared might mean her downfall.

Louis, having descended the Petit Escalier du Roi, was walking across the Salle des Gardes in the flickering light of the *flambeaux* when a man pushed his way through the line of Swiss Guards and struck him a blow below the ribs. No one was quite sure what had happened until the king put his hand to his side and, taking it away, saw that it was covered with blood. "It's that man there with his hat on," cried the Duc de Richelieu, pointing to the assailant who had made no attempt to escape but had rejoined the crowd and stood looking upon the group of men clustered around the king.

Insisting that he was quite capable of walking back up the stairs, Louis returned to the Petits Appartements — but having reached them, he felt faint. Sup-

posing the dagger had been poisoned, the king feared that he was going to die. Although the wound was not a deep one, the doctor, too, thought that he might have been poisoned, for the knife was such as a poisoner might have used — a penknife with the smaller of the two blades open. When Louis had confessed, his daughters came into the room and, at the sight of their father lying on the blood-soaked bed, they fainted. Then the queen came and she also fainted. The dauphin began to cry. Mme. de Pompadour, who had been at Trianon when the attack had been made, dashed back to the palace but was not admitted to the room.

For days, while the king slowly recovered, Mme. de Pompadour had no word from him, and her enemies began to hope that — having confessed his sins — he would do to her what he had failed to do to the Duchesse de Châteauroux after his illness at Metz. They were disappointed: far from abandoning her, the king — by the time that his assailant, Robert François Damiens, an unbalanced servant from Artois, had been tried, condemned, and tortured to death — seemed on better terms than ever with Mme. de Pompadour. Soon they were making plans together for yet further renovation, redecoration, and building at Versailles.

Their favorite project was the creation of a new country house in the gardens at Trianon where they could enjoy the same privacy and rustic pleasures that they had known at the Hermitage, but in grander style. This Petit Trianon was to be a much more simple and intimate house than Louis XIV's imposing Trianon de Marbre, but it was to have a formal elegance befitting the new taste for classical purity. In close cooperation with the king and Mme. de Pompadour, Jacques Ange

Gabriel began to make plans and sketches for his masterpiece. By the end of 1762 the walls of honey-colored stone were taking shape. The king frequently came over from the palace to keep a watch on the building's progress, to see the cows, the poultry, pigeons, and sheep in the nearby farmyard, to discuss the layout of the gardens with his *jardinier-fleuriste,* Claude Richard, and to inspect the beds where grew every known variety of strawberry.

Yet Mme. de Pompadour was not able to accompany him on these visits as often as she had in the days when he cooked their supper at the Hermitage, for her health was failing. Before the Petit Trianon was finished, she fell seriously ill.

One evening in 1764, while she was staying at Choisy, the hunting lodge that Gabriel had altered and enlarged for the king, she was attacked by so fierce a headache that she did not know where she was and had to be guided back to her room and put to bed — to what her doctors feared next day would be her deathbed. However, she rallied sufficiently for the king to give instructions for her to be moved to Versailles, though he did not believe she could recover and traditionally only members of the royal family were allowed to die in the palace.

Upon her arrival at the palace, she suffered a relapse, and the king knew that the end must be near. For almost twenty years they had shared an "unshakable friendship," and he was overwhelmed with grief at the thought of losing her. Louis remained by her bedside for hours on end, looking upon her tired, rouged face. She sat in a chair as her lungs were congested and she could not breathe lying down. Whenever anyone came

Coolly dignified and elegantly attired, Mme. de Pompadour (opposite) was portrayed by Quentin de La Tour surrounded by the works of art and learning she so avidly patronized during her long reign as Louis XV's mistress. Though she was never replaced in the king's heart, Pompadour's place in his bed was eventually given over to a series of other ladies — including the callipygian morsel below, Mlle. Louise O'Murphy, whom François Boucher has depicted sprawled across a Louis XV sofa. But despite her obvious charms, even Mlle. O'Murphy did not long remain a royal favorite; for the king she was, at bottom, but a passing fancy.

into the room, she smiled at him and, although she was obviously in great pain, she did not complain. At last, when she felt death approaching, she asked the king if he thought the time had come for her to confess. He knew that this would mean his leaving her, but he said he thought she must. So Louis tenderly wished her good-bye and went up to his apartments.

He could not sleep that night, nor for several nights after her death. On the evening of her funeral — which court etiquette forbade him to attend — he walked out of the Cabinet Intime and onto the balcony overlooking the Place d'Armes and stood there in the pouring rain watching the slow cortege making its way toward Paris. When he came back into the room, tears were falling down his cheeks. To his Valet of the Bedchamber he murmured, "That was the only tribute I am able to pay her."

It was a sad time for France as well as for Louis. The year before the Seven Years' War had ended and in it the country had suffered a series of disastrous defeats. In 1757 Frederick the Great had defeated the Prince de Soubise at Rossbach; in 1759 British troops under General Wolfe conquered Quebec; and in 1761 the Comte de Lally was obliged to surrender at Pondicherry. The French Mediterranean fleet was crippled, and the Atlantic fleet was virtually destroyed. By the Peace of Paris of 1763 France was evicted from India and her power in Canada was ended. Senegal in Africa and Minorca in the Mediterranean both passed to England.

Louis XV himself never fully recovered from the loss of Mme. de Pompadour — nor did Versailles. Because he was so lonely without her, he established an-

other mistress in her place, but she was not the gifted
woman that Mme. de Pompadour had been. It was
said of her that she would never have lasted a month
at Versailles if her predecessor had survived but would
have been discarded, like all those prostitutes who
were installed at the Parc aux Cerfs.

Yet the Comtesse du Barry was very beautiful; no
one denied that. Also, she was amusing and she was
young. On the day of her presentation at Versailles in
1768 she was twenty-two; the king was fifty-nine and
had but five years left to live. The illegitimate daughter of a poor woman of Vaucouleurs, she had received
the scantiest of educations and had worked in a mil-
liner's shop and as a prostitute before becoming the
mistress of the Chevalier Jean du Barry. The chevalier
— being married himself — married her off to his
brother, the Comte du Barry, in order to facilitate her
progress at court and thus further his own ambitions.
In this he was entirely successful, for the king became
utterly infatuated with her and denied her nothing.

Louis never seemed entirely happy with Mme. du
Barry, however, and was never able to enjoy her company in the way he had enjoyed that of Mme. de Pompadour. Only at the Petit Trianon was he able to
capture some of the pleasure of the past. This delightful house was now finished, decorated, and furnished,
and the king spent as much time there as he could.
Apart from the Salle des Gardes and a billiard room,
the ground floor was taken up with offices and kitchens.
The main living quarters, including two dining rooms,
a Grand Salon de Compagnie, the Cabinet du Roi, and
a botanical library, were on the upper floors and commanded fine views over the gardens. Indeed, the gar-

dens seemed almost to enter the house, for the walls
of these upper floors were all covered with floral motifs, with intricately carved — and accurately observed
— lilacs and roses, with strawberries, apples, and pears.
In the main dining room, so that the privacy of the
king's suppers might not be disturbed by the presence
of servants, the tables could be lowered through the
floor into the kitchens where they were piled with food
and sent gliding up again by means of counterweights.

The king was at the Petit Trianon in April 1774
when it was noticed by the light of a candle as he bent
over a table that his cheeks were blotched with red
marks. He had contracted smallpox. At sixty-four, with
a constitution weakened by excess, he was not expected
to recover.

Louis wanted to die at the Petit Trianon, but he was
advised that the setting was inappropriate: he would
have to be moved back to the palace. So the doctors
wrapped him up in a cloak and, feverish though he
was, carried him down to a waiting coach. He died on
May 10 in the middle of the afternoon. No sooner had
the scabbed eyes closed in the black and swollen face
than the bossy Comtesse de Noailles, her principal lady-
in-waiting, bustled down the corridor to tell the dauphine that she was Queen of France.

VI
Monarchy at the Abyss

The new queen was Marie Antoinette, daughter of the Empress Maria Theresa of Austria and sister of the young Emperor Joseph II. She had come to Versailles from Vienna four years earlier, when she was fifteen, and had married the dauphin in the sunlit white stone chapel a few days after her arrival. She was a charming child, alert, intelligent, affectionate; and although her forehead was too high, her face too long, and her lower lip too prominent for her to be considered beautiful, there was a vivacity about Marie Antoinette's features and a captivating grace about her movements.

The bridegroom had no such grace or vivacity. He was Louis XV's grandson, his father having died when he was eleven. A dull youth of sixteen, ungainly and sullen, he appeared to take little interest in life when he was not out hunting and spent much of his time in the company of carpenters and masons, though he displayed scant skill at their trades. He seemed at his happiest when eating. "What is for breakfast?" he would ask upon waking and, upon being told, would usually declare it was not enough. He had been known to consume four cutlets, a chicken, a plateful of ham, a half dozen eggs in sauce, and a bottle and a half of champagne before setting out to hunt.

On the day of his marriage the future Louis XVI walked to the chapel looking cross and embarrassed in his diamond-studded suit, holding hands reluctantly with his fresh young bride. Throughout the long ceremony, which was conducted by the Archbishop of Reims, he appeared to be as gloomily apprehensive as she was expectant and excited. That evening, as though to complement his mood, there was a dreadful thunderstorm. Only during the banquet did he seem to

become momentarily at ease, putting his head down and eating ravenously. His grandfather admonished him gently: "You really should not stuff yourself so on a night like this." "Why not?" the boy answered in his loud voice. "I always sleep better after a good meal." Despite the bridegroom's boorish behavior, the celebrations of the *Festin Royal* that night at Versailles were an undoubted success.

The banquet was held in the recently completed Salle de Spectacle, or Opéra, a great theater near the reservoir, designed to become the permanent setting for such festivities. Ever since the court of Louis XIV had moved to Versailles, temporary structures had been erected at enormous expense, only to be demolished when the function for which they had been created was over. For the celebrations in honor of the marriage of the dauphin's father, for instance, a magnificent ballroom had been built in the Grande Écurie. The Salle de Spectacle, however, designed by Gabriel in 1748 but for many years unrealized, was meant to last. Painted to resemble marble and lighted by vast chandeliers whose light was reflected in the mirrors set into the colonnades, it was a delightful and impressive building with a ceiling painted by Durameau.

The royal family's table — where the bridegroom ate so gluttonously and the bride scarcely at all — had been set in the middle of the floor surrounded by a balustrade. Beyond the balustrade sat the guests in tiers of boxes, their jewels and the silks and satins of their costumes shining in the candlelight. On the stage almost two hundred musicians competed with the constant buzz of conversation. After the meal there was gambling in the Galerie des Glaces where the Duc

de Croÿ was enthralled by the gorgeous dresses glittering in the light reflected by the tall mirrors.

At midnight the bride and bridegroom were conducted to their bedchambers. The dauphin was handed his nightgown by the king, the dauphine took hers from the Duchesse de Chartres; the Archbishop of Reims blessed the bed. But the bride slept alone. The next morning her husband came into Marie Antoinette's room, asked her abruptly, "Did you sleep," received the answer "Yes," and without another word he went out hunting.

The wedding celebrations continued for ten days: there was a ball and a performance of Lully's *Perseus* in the Salle de Spectacle, now an opera house once more; there was a marvelous fireworks display to rival any given in the time of Louis XIV, a display that was started by the king himself hurling a flaming spear through one of the open windows of the Galerie des Glaces and which was concluded by a "girande of twenty thousand rockets."

After the fireworks display the Bassin d'Apollon — surrounded by glittering arcades and trellises, arches and obelisks — was so brilliantly illuminated that, as one spectator said, "everything that one reads of Fairyland would give but an imperfect idea of this night at Versailles" during which 200,000 people from Paris and the countryside around danced all night by the light of the colored lamps. "The immense park," this observer continued, "illuminated throughout its entire extent, was far more brilliant than when lit by the sun in all its splendor."

Yet for Marie Antoinette these days were far from happy ones. Her husband took not the least interest in her, and although the king was kind to her, she was inevitably caught up in the intrigues of the women who surrounded him. Moreover, her daily life at Versailles was not likely to keep a lively young girl amused.

She got out of bed between nine and ten o'clock, made a courtesy call upon her aunts after breakfast, then had her hair done before receiving visitors at noon. Mass followed, then dinner with the dauphin who rarely spoke to her; while he went out — usually hunting — she was left alone in her private apartments to read, to write to her family, or to do her needlework. At three she was required to make another visit to her aunts, then to undergo religious instruction and a serious conversation and lessons with her tutor, the Abbé de Vermond. These studies were followed by lessons on the clavichord and the harp — though her husband had told her he did not like music — after which she went out for an airing in the park. Supper was at nine, and after supper she had to wait up in case the king wanted to see her; if he had not arrived by eleven she went to bed. Sometimes there was a play or an opera; occasionally she acted in a play with her brothers-in-law and their wives. But this was not very enjoyable, as her husband was the only member of the audience and a completely silent one at that, not infrequently fast asleep by the end of the performance.

She did not dislike the dauphin, though; her disdain was mixed with a kind of affection. Much of his rudeness and gaucheries could be attributed to shyness and lack of confidence; perhaps when they grew to know each other better, he would be more at ease with her. Certainly after the death of his grandfather in 1774, he seemed to take on a new authority — and

The marriage of the dauphin to Marie Antoinette, the Archduchess of Austria, was already arranged when the future Louis XVI was first introduced to his bride. In the engraving at left the groom-to-be, standing beside his grandfather, Louis XV (seated), is shown a portrait of his intended. For the wedding a splendid new entertainment room was added to Versailles' north wing. The last important addition to the château, the Opéra, or Salle de Spectacle (opposite), was made of gilded and marbleized wood. With adjustments in the floor level it served either as a theater, a ballroom, or a banquet hall.

she could finally escape from the restraints of the palace to the informal delights of the Petit Trianon, which her husband, shortly after his accession as King Louis XVI, had given her.

It was, wrote the Empress Maria Theresa, a "charming present"; but she hoped that her daughter would not be prompted by it to indulge in "too great expense." Everything depended upon things going well at the start. A king of twenty and a queen of nineteen: this held "the promise of much happiness"; but she must not abuse her privileges.

Marie Antoinette had little patience with such advice. She and the younger members of the court looked forward now to bringing a breath of fresh air into the stuffy corridors of Versailles. They were "happy to scoff at the old-fashioned ways, the grave etiquette of our elders," wrote one of these young courtiers, the Comte de Ségur. "Anything that was long established seemed to us tiresome and ridiculous. . . . We walked upon a carpet of flowers." The carpet, he added, writing in the knowledge of what followed those halcyon days, "covered an abyss."

The queen herself, careless of the future, was constantly provoked by the rigid decorum of the staid and pompous Comtesse de Noailles, "Madame l'Etiquette," to whom a pin misplaced on a court gown was a tragedy. This lady was insistent that no minutia of court tradition or etiquette should ever be altered or disregarded. In consequence, the queen's daily routine soon became a tiresome burden to her. It was considered essential, for instance, that her chemise be handed to her in the morning when she was dressing by her *dame d'honneur;* if a royal princess were present, however, the chemise had first to be handed to her, and then it became her duty to present it to the queen.

One morning as the dressing ceremony was about to begin, there was a scratch at the door and the Duchesse d'Orléans was admitted. The duchess took the chemise, but before she could hand it on there was a second scratch announcing the arrival of the Comtesse de Provence, who had precedence over the duchess. The chemise must therefore be given to her; but it could not be handed directly from one of the royal ladies to another, so it had to pass through the hands of the *dame d'honneur.* While these movements were being performed with the correct choreographic emphasis, the queen stood shivering in the cold and drafty room, murmuring to herself, *"C'est odieux!"*

Marie Antoinette had never been a patient young woman and as queen was developing into a willful and selfish one. She was determined to get her own way and usually did so. Refusing to be bound by her duties and obligations as Queen of France, she made the king and the court well aware that she would live — so far as it was possible at Versailles — as a private citizen.

For his part, the king was incapable of behaving like a monarch. With his ministers and in council he appeared ill at ease, incompetent, and ill-informed, though he worked much harder to comprehend their problems than his grandfather had ever done. Louis found it impossible to remain still during a conversation but shuffled his feet nervously or fidgeted in his chair. With those whom he knew well he would wrestle and box like a rough boy, or advance upon them step by step so that they had to back against the wall and, when they had reached it, he would only laugh and

turn away. At his *coucher* he had been seen to throw his blue ribband playfully but forcefully in the face of a solemn courtier, to make a face and run away when his nightgown was thrown at him, to walk up and down with his breeches hanging around his ankles, scratching himself, supposing himself amusing rather than merely undignified.

As he walked about the palace he looked less like a king than a "peasant waddling behind a plough"; sometimes he could be seen kneeling down in front of a door trying to get a key he had made in his forge to turn a difficult lock.

Louis did have interests other than hunting and eating, but they were not enduring. His skill as a locksmith was more imagined than real; his reading of books — and he read a great many — was cursory and unavailing. He did, however, build a beautiful library for which much was forgiven him. Using one of the rooms occupied by Mme. de Pompadour in her later years, instructing Gabriel as designer and Antoine Rousseau as the executive artist, he produced a lovely room in the new style that came to be known by his title, Louis Seize. It was his favorite room in the whole palace; here he would sit, with his back to the shelves and the lovely painted carvings in the panels between them, looking out of the window at the people and the carriages milling about in the courtyard outside.

As time passed this clumsy, ponderous, rough, good-natured young man grew ever more fond of his wife, a fascinating creature for all her faults and indiscretions. He paid her gambling debts; he indulged her passion for diamonds; he even smiled and forgave her when she mocked him, making no secret of her preference for men wittier and livelier than he. Yet there was a sadness in the smile and everyone at court knew why. After several years of marriage, their union had yet to be consummated. The king had a physical abnormality that made him nearly impotent and the queen used this as an excuse to keep him out of her bed.

One evening, while Louis was relating a hunting story, Marie Antoinette attempted to alleviate her boredom by flicking pellets of bread at him. "What would you do," he asked the Minister of War who was sitting nearby, "if you were in the field and the enemy kept peppering you like this?" "Sire," replied the minister, without reflecting on the *double entendre,* "I should spike their cannon." Then, realizing how his words might be interpreted, he blushed and turned away. Such embarrassing incidents were frequent.

Satirical verses and lampoons, jokes and cartoons, were passed about the court; the king was upbraided for his timidity; the queen, the already disliked Austrian, was jeered at by the ignorant women of Versailles for being barren. She had a passage made between her own apartments and those of the king so that he did not have to walk across the public rooms to reach her. But still Louis was unable to fulfill his marital obligations to Marie Antoinette and his royal duty to France of producing an heir.

Because of her intimate friendship with the charming and gorgeous Princesse de Lamballe — who became her *dame d'atours* after the longed-for departure of the Comtesse de Noailles — and then with the even more desirable Comtesse de Polignac, it was said that the queen compensated herself for the king's incapacity by illicit affairs not only with handsome young men but

Soon after his accession to the throne in 1774, Louis XVI, an avid reader, commissioned Jacques Ange Gabriel, the architect who designed the Petit Trianon, to create an elegant library at Versailles. Working toward the classical simplicity of his earlier triumph, Gabriel designed a room (right) of white and gold, its quiet ornamentation and simple gilded paneling epitomizing the style that soon became known as Louis Seize.

the seclusion of the private world that she was making for herself at Versailles.

Soon after her first baby was born the queen began to rebuild her Petits Cabinets, disdaining all protests about the lack of money in the building fund, changing her mind repeatedly about color schemes and styles, driving the architects and workmen frantic with her sudden whims and fancies. She altered the library, filling the shelves with as many false backs as real volumes, since books for her were more desirable as a form of decoration than instruction. She altered the octagonal room known as the Méridienne, covering the walls with mirrors and getting the designer Richard Mique, and the young Rousseau brothers, sons of Antoine, to decorate the panels between them with symbols to celebrate the birth of the dauphin, which had occurred in October 1781. In this room she tried on her enormous wigs, selected her jewels, held long discussions with her dressmaker, Rose Bertin, whose shop was in the rue Saint-Honoré, and chose the dresses she would wear each day at mass by sticking a pin in a book that contained patterns of all those she possessed.

The larger room nearby, the Cabinet Intérieur — the name of which was changed to the Cabinet Doré after it had been completely redecorated and its panels ornamented with gilt carvings — was the room in which the queen received her visitors. But neither this room nor any of the other Petits Cabinets of the queen were ever open to the public, as were those of the king whenever he was not in residence. Indeed, so determined was Marie Antoinette to live a private life — to be herself, as she so often put it, and not to be stared at as a queen — that she spent increasingly less

The decaying state of the gardens at Versailles, along with the newly fashionable desire to return to nature, prompted Louis XVI to spend enormous amounts of money on replanting many of the gardens and transforming others into studied imitations of rural landscapes. Hubert Robert's painting (left, below) presents a view of the work near the château, where one dead tree is being pulled down while others are put to the saw. Marie Antoinette's Temple of Love, built on an artificial island in an artificial stream, is shown at left. Nearby, hills were thrown up, a lake dug, and a grotto with a gushing cascade installed — all for the queen's pleasure. The dainty little Belvédère (right) dominates the Arcadian scene.
    Overleaf:
During summertime fetes the gardens at the Petit Trianon were lighted by thousands of flaming torches, as in this painting by Châtelet, bathing the grottoes and the Belvédère in a weird ethereal light.

time in the palace and was more and more to be found with her chosen friends at the Petit Trianon. Versailles was too much like a town; Marly was too grand and too exposed; but the Trianon offered her just the seclusion she wanted.

It also, unfortunately, offered her scope for spending more money. There was little she could do to the house itself, for it had so recently and so exquisitely been finished, so she contented herself with decorating in the new style her small boudoir behind her bedroom. But there was much to be done in the garden. "We must get back to nature," her friend, the Prince de Ligne, had said to her. "We have had enough of formal gardens. Trianon must be an arcadia." These were her views entirely, and she set to work with a will, appointing Mique and the Comte de Caraman, whose garden in Paris was a delight, as her sole advisers.

The indulgent king ordered that everything the queen wanted should be provided "with all the care and speed possible."

Although the Superintendent of Buildings attempted to curb and control the queen's expenditure, he failed to do so. She got her own way as usual and was soon criticizing the models of painted wood and wax that were produced for her inspection and approval. As the Comte Mercy d'Argenteau said, people were growing very much concerned at the great expense that she was incurring and threatening to incur.

Miniature ranges of hills were thrown up, lakes were dug, smooth green lawns were laid, grottoes were built, waterfalls created, and an immensely expensive Chinese Pavilion with a blue and gold canopy appeared in front of the Petit Trianon's windows. This pavilion could be made to revolve by men turning levers in a hole beneath it; the queen and her friends, sitting on a platform in seats shaped like peacocks or mandarins, attempted to throw pegs through the rings that dangled from the canopy as they were whirled dizzily around and around.

On an artificial plateau overlooking the lake there was erected an elaborate, octagonal stone summerhouse, known as the Belvédère, finely carved on the outside and with paintings inside by Le Riche and Lagrenée. On a flower-covered island in the river that led through green meadows beyond the lake was a stately temple, the Temple d'Amour, a shallow cupola supported by twelve tall columns that rose above Bouchardon's statue of Venus. Behind the temple and on either side of it were all manner of exotic trees and shrubs collected from every corner of the world; swans glided down the river; birds sang overhead.

In the lovely gardens of the Petit Trianon there was also a theater where the queen and her small, intimate circle of friends gave occasional performances for privileged audiences, usually limited to members of the royal family and the queen's servants, much to the annoyance of other members of the court. The plays performed ranged from Jean Jacques Rousseau's *Le Devin du Village* — in which the queen played one of her favorite parts, that of Colette, the ordinary village girl — to Jean François Marmontel's *Dormeur Réveillé*. The latter play was given for the benefit of King Gustavus III of Sweden, who was presented with a copy of the script bound in green leather and embossed in gold with the arms of the Swedish royal house; the other members of the audience were pre-

three
Grand
and a
Infant
and de
difficu
of the

The
while
At firs
If he
least
powde
"No,
shed!"
tion t
peatin
nothi

Th
the sl
swarn
fishwi
Halle
tear h
Bread
cries
fell to

Th
there
swere

In
fright
Antoi

Royale and began to mount the staircase to the queen's room. The queen was awakened by the shouts: "Death to the Austrian. Where is she? We'll wring the whore's neck! We'll tear her heart out!"

In the anteroom one of the guards was vainly struggling to bar the door with his musket. "Save the queen!" he shouted to her ladies-in-waiting, the blood pouring down his face. "They are going to kill her!"

The queen jumped out of bed, put on her petticoat and clasped a cape about her shoulders when her two ladies urged her to run without bothering to dress. The three fled through the Petits Cabinets, hastily locking the doors behind them, to the door that led into the Salon de l'Oeil de Boeuf and the safety of the king's apartments. It was locked on the inside.

The women beat on the door with their fists and screamed for help. There was no answer.

The king, aroused by the uproar, had run through a secret passage in the *entresol* of the Salon de l'Oeil de Boeuf to the queen's bedroom. Seeing the bed empty, he had run back again and as he ran one of his *Valets de la Garderobe* at last unlocked the door to admit the queen and her ladies. They ran into the king's empty bedroom where a candle still flickered on a table. The queen picked up the candlestick and was about to run off in search of her son when the king appeared with the dauphin in his arms. At sight of them she regained her composure; the children's governess said that she now appeared quite unmoved by her ordeal; "her countenance was sad but calm."

Outside the mob was fighting and plundering, parading the severed heads of two guards about the courtyards on pikes. The Marquis de Lafayette arrived with

Finding an unlocked gate at Versailles, the Paris mob surged through the château on the morning of October 6, 1789, intent on murdering the hated Marie Antoinette, whom they nicknamed Madame Déficit. A faithful servant held the crowd back long enough for the queen to escape. Fleeing through the door shown opposite, she and her children found momentary refuge in the king's apartments. That day, in an attempt to placate the mob, the king appeared on the balcony overlooking the Cour de Marbre (below). Compelled to accompany the revolutionaries back to Paris, Louis and his family were forcibly detained in the city and never saw Versailles again. The king was finally deposed in September 1792 and executed in January 1793. Marie Antoinette followed him to the guillotine a few months later.

his troops, attempted to quell the riot, and told the king and queen that order could only be restored if they showed themselves to the crowd before accompanying him back to Paris. To shouts of "The king to Paris! The king to Paris!" Louis went out onto the balcony first. There were a few cheers.

Then the queen came out holding the dauphin by one hand and his sister by the other. "No children! No children!" the mob shouted. "The queen alone!"

She ushered the children back into the room and stood there alone, looking down at the upturned faces in the Cour Royale. Several muskets were pointed at her. She stood quite still, her head erect, apparently unaffected by the scene. Her calm, defiant bravery was impressive and strangely moving. Slowly the muskets were lowered. She turned away and walked back into the room and then across to her Petits Cabinets. At last, she sat down and began to cry.

Already there were carts and carriages in the courtyards as preparations were made to move the royal family to the Tuileries; soon they rolled out of the Cour des Ministres, into the Place d'Armes, and off to Paris, escorted by the troops and the shouting rabble. The royal coach was surrounded by women who jumped onto the backs of soldiers, picked off their hats and put them on their own heads, shouting insults. At ten o'clock at night the slow procession reached the Tuileries, and the royal family was taken into the cold, unfurnished rooms of the dilapidated palace. The dauphin sleepily murmured, "It's very ugly here, mother."

At Versailles the palace they had left was locked and shuttered, overcast, in the words of the Marquise de La Tour du Pin, by "a ghastly solitude."

Marie Antoinette left no more fitting symbol of her reign than the Hameau, or hamlet, which she had built in a distant corner of the palace grounds. A monument of extravagant simplicity, the toy village had its own thatched cottages, a dairy barn with marble walls and floors and a prize herd of Swiss cows, and a picturesque watermill (below), where the village maidens did their washing and the village peasants ground their corn. For the queen there was a vine-covered cottage (opposite), complete with cracked plaster and worm-ridden beams, all carefully created at great expense to give the proper appearance of dilapidation. Yet the rooms inside were as lavish and elegant as the rooms at the grand château, having been adorned with tapestries and carpets and flowerpots of the finest porcelain. Here, without too much discomfort, the queen could escape from the world, pretending she was merely the wife of a country squire. In the portrait at right the queen, humbly attired in lace and feathers, walks with her children in the garden of the Petit Trianon. The Temple of Love is in the background.

into the king's bedchamber, dressing-room, etc. in all of which were numbers of people, and many of them indifferently clad." Horace Walpole made similar comments: "In the colonnades, upon the staircase, nay in the antechambers of the royal family, there are people selling all sorts of wares. While we were waiting in the dauphin's sumptuous bedchamber, till his dressing-room door should be opened, two fellows were sweeping it, and dancing about in sabots to rub the floor."

The same sort of incongruous scenes were to be witnessed in the chapel, where "the king [Louis XVI] laughed and spied at the ladies; every eye was fixed on the personages of the court . . . while the priest, who in the meantime went on in the exercise of his office, was unheeded by all present. Even when the Host was lifted up, none observed it; and if the people knelt, it was because they were admonished by the ringing of the bell; and, even in that attitude, all were endeavoring to get a glimpse of the king."

Although Versailles was naturally on the itinerary of every young gentleman who entered France on the first stages of his Grand Tour of Europe, surprisingly few of these tourists were deeply impressed by their visit. For their benefit a *coche d'osier,* designed to carry sixteen passengers, left Paris twice every day from the rue Saint-Niçaise. They entered the coach in high expectation, carrying their copy of the relevant volume of Nugent's *The Grand Tour Containing An Exact Description of . . . The Remarkable Places of Europe,* the most celebrated guidebook of the time, which described Versailles as "one of the finest palaces of the world."

But most of these tourists were — or, at least, con-

*Though Versailles survived the Revolution almost
intact, it quickly began falling into disrepair.
Early in the 1830's Louis Philippe, the "Bourgeois
King," decided to rescue the home of his ancestors.
With good intentions but execrable taste, he had
many of Versailles' finest interiors destroyed so
that the château might be turned into a museum
dedicated "to all the glories of France." Below,
the king is shown amidst a throng at the
inauguration of the new museum in 1837.
Meantime, the château continued to influence the
design of noble houses throughout Europe, as it
had during the reign of the Sun King, casting
its spell upon Englishmen viewing the gardens
and façade of Montagu House in London (right).*

fessed themselves to be — disappointed, agreeing with Horace Walpole that Versailles was, after all, "a lumber of littleness, composed of black brick, stuck full of bad old busts, and fringed with gold rails." Dr. Johnson, who came to Versailles with his friends, the Thrales, also professed himself to be not much impressed and recorded briefly in his diary: "To Versailles, a mean town. Carriages of business passing. Mean shops against the wall. The palace of great extent. — The front long. . . ." Most of the rest of his laconic account is taken up with the animals in the menagerie.

Another Englishman, even more prejudiced against things French and in favor of things English, Lord Macaulay, doubted "whether there be anywhere any single architectural composition of equal extent . . . yet there are a dozen country houses of private individuals in England alone which have a greater air of majesty and splendor than this huge quarry."

Nevertheless, there were visitors enough who were sufficiently impressed by the glories of Versailles to return home determined to use it as a model for a palace or country house of their own. In England, in the late seventeenth and early eighteenth centuries, several country houses were built by rich young men who had fallen under the spell of Versailles during their years abroad. Montagu House in Bloomsbury, designed by Robert Hooke as a London house for Ralph, Duke of Montagu — who for several years was British Ambassador at the Court of Louis XIV — was a characteristic example. So was Boughton House in Northamptonshire, the Duke of Montagu's magnificent country house which, as contemporaries noted, was

"contrived after the model of Versailles." So, too, was Petworth House in Sussex, the immense mansion built between 1688 and 1696 for Charles Seymour, sixth Duke of Somerset; while the great marble entrance hall at Castle Howard, the Yorkshire mansion of the third Earl of Carlisle, was certainly inspired by the work of Louis XIV's architect, Louis Le Vau.

The interiors of these and many other houses were decorated throughout by French craftsmen and artists; several of them, like the great master of wrought-iron-work Jean Tijou, were Huguenots exiled by Louis XIV's ill-advised revocation of the Edict of Nantes. At Montagu House the interior decoration was entirely entrusted to Rousseau, Lafosse, and Jean Baptiste Monnoyer.

As with the buildings and interiors, so it was with the gardens: the influence of Versailles was unmistakable until the taste for the more natural landscapes of "Capability" Brown and Humphry Repton made Lenôtre's neatness, order, and regularity unfashionable. Lenôtre himself was called over to England to advise Charles II upon the layout of the royal park at St. James's; and the gardens at Hampton Court Palace were redesigned in the popular French style.

It was on the Continent, however, that the influence of Versailles was most widespread. Peter the Great, who had stayed in the palace during his foreign tour, took back to Russia with him the architect Le Blond who drew up designs for the tsar's palace, Peterhof, which was begun in 1720. The services of Louis XIV's own architect, Robert de Cotte, were called upon by lesser foreign rulers and autocrats from the Elector of Cologne to the Prince von Thurn und Taxis. Indeed, there was scarcely a princeling in all Germany who did not feel himself deprived until he possessed a palace on the model of Versailles, furnished and decorated in the French taste, with a garden in the style of Lenôtre, and with his courtiers, attendants, courtesans, cooks, and artists trained to behave, to serve, and to perform in the French manner. So it was that along the Rhine, the Meuse, and the Moselle, in The Palatinate and Wittenburg, in Cologne and Trèves, Brunswick and Hesse, there arose palaces that owed their inspiration to Le Vau, de Cotte, and Mansart, and to the kings of France who had been their patrons.

It was an influence that was slow to die. When the nineteenth century was far advanced, the enormously rich Baron Ferdinand de Rothschild elected to build a vast mansion in the style of Versailles in a quiet corner of the English countryside in Buckinghamshire. The house was designed by the French architect Destailleur and the grounds were laid out by the French landscape gardener Lainé. While Waddesdon Manor was being built, an even more ambitious project was devised by King Ludwig II of Bavaria who decided to construct, on a reduced scale, a replica of Versailles on the island of Herrenchiemsee. At the most extravagant cost, Ludwig's ambition was largely achieved and — before he was declared insane — the king's chief pleasure was to wander alone from apartment to apartment in his vast private museum, lost in dreams of past grandeur.

Although Versailles itself had become a museum, it was still occasionally called upon to fulfill its original function. In 1856, for instance, Queen Victoria was entertained there by her ally in the recently ended Crimean War, Napoleon III. A ball was given in the Galerie des Glaces followed by supper in the Salle de Spectacle; and the English queen, delighted by a fireworks display in the best Versailles manner, was particularly pleased by the *pièce de résistance,* a set piece of her own great palace, Windsor Castle.

Soon, however, Versailles once more had to face sad days. In the Franco-Prussian War, which broke out in 1870, the palace was used as the Prussian military headquarters; and it was in the Galerie des Glaces, on January 18, 1871, that Wilhelm I was proclaimed emperor of a united Germany. During the subsequent take-over of Paris by the Commune, the National Assembly and the new republican government fled to Versailles. The Galerie des Glaces was divided into cubicles and used as a dormitory; the Salle de Spectacle — Durameau's ceiling painting rolled up and stored and replaced by a skylight — served as the chamber of the senate; and ministries were installed in the various suites of apartments in the palace itself.

The government returned to Paris in 1879, but thirty-five years later another war — World War I — cast its shadow over the palace. The shadow lifted when the Treaty of Versailles, by which France and her victorious allies humbled Germany, was signed in the Galerie des Glaces on June 28, 1919. Inevitably there was another war a generation later, and the Germans returned once more. When *that* war was over at last, the reconstruction of Versailles as one of the greatest palaces of the world could begin in earnest.

The guidelines to be followed in the execution of this great work had already been set. In 1887 a young man named Pierre de Nolhac, whose application to join the staff of a museum of higher prestige had been

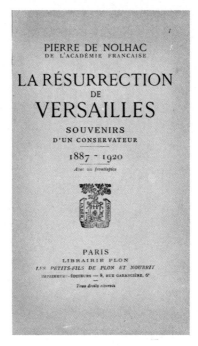

PIERRE DE NOLHAC
DE L'ACADÉMIE FRANÇAISE

LA RÉSURRECTION
DE
VERSAILLES
SOUVENIRS
D'UN CONSERVATEUR
1887 - 1920
Avec un frontispice

PARIS
LIBRAIRIE PLON
LES PETITS-FILS DE PLON ET NOURRIT
IMPRIMEURS-ÉDITEURS — 8, RUE GARANCIÈRE, 6e
Tous droits réservés

turned down, was offered an appointment at Versailles. He reluctantly accepted it, for Versailles was known to be an ill-run museum with its sparse and dusty exhibits shown in dull galleries from which all past splendors had been effaced. Nolhac's suggestions for cleaning and rearranging these exhibits, and for restoring the rooms in which they were housed, were met with the blank indifference of his complacent and indolent superiors.

In time, however, Nolhac was promoted in the hierarchy of his department and, as curator of Versailles from 1892 to 1920, was enabled to bring his formidable gifts to bear upon the regeneration of the palace. By prolonged and meticulous examination of all the available documents, he first of all reconstructed the topography of the palace as it had existed in the days before the Revolution. He discovered the former uses of storerooms and cupboards, of offices and cloakrooms, and established, for example, that the room in which the museum's cleaning staff kept their mops and brushes had once been Louis XV's delicately painted bathroom.

Having established the original topography of the palace, Nolhac then began restoring its previous decoration: by repainting, regilding, and revarnishing rooms in accordance with the architects' designs discovered in the National Archives; by replacing features, or replicas of features, that had been removed; and by removing extraneous elements that later generations had added. As the work progressed — and as Nolhac published books about Versailles, lectured about it, aroused a new enthusiasm for its forgotten or submerged treasures — a fresh interest in the palace of Versailles was gradually engendered.

The reformation was slow, for there was never enough money to carry out in full the ambitious schemes of Nolhac and his successors; even the generosity of John D. Rockefeller, Jr., who donated $700,000 for the repair and restoration of Versailles, was insufficient to meet the full cost. But the work continues: Marie Antoinette's theater as well as the Petit and Grand Trianons, the Salle de Spectacle, the Galerie des Glaces, and the Chapel have all now been restored to their pristine charm and magnificence. And there, as elsewhere at Versailles, in grand apartments and little cabinets, in cobbled courtyards and beside the waters of the gardens, the modern visitor feels himself surrounded by ghosts, the vanished figures of the *ancien régime*.

To two English ladies, one August afternoon in the early part of the present century, these ghosts seemed to materialize. One of the ladies, Miss Charlotte Moberly, was principal of an Oxford college; the other, Miss Eleanor Jourdain, was the headmistress of a girls' school. They were both the daughters of Church of England clergymen, both orthodox Anglicans themselves, both highly intelligent and trustworthy; they shared a horror of spiritualism and had never had any sort of psychic experience. After some days of sight-seeing in Paris, they decided to visit Versailles, although they had very vague ideas as to what there was to be seen there; as they later admitted, their knowledge of French history was "limited to the very little."

Having gone over the palace, Miss Moberly suggested that they take a walk in the gardens. Following a path marked on the map in their guidebook, talking about England and their friends at home, they passed what they supposed was the Grand Trianon. Gradually, although they had both left the palace in the best of spirits, an extraordinary feeling of depression came over Miss Moberly, a feeling that "steadily deepened" and "became quite overbearing." She tried to conceal this from her friend, but Miss Jourdain shared it. "There was a feeling of depression and loneliness about the place," Miss Jourdain recorded afterward. "I began to feel as if I were walking in my sleep; the heavy dreaminess was oppressive."

They came upon strange figures in strange clothes, two men in long grayish-green coats and small three-cornered hats whom they took to be officials or, because of a nearby wheelbarrow and a pointed spade, gardeners perhaps. Miss Jourdain asked the way, and was told to go straight on in such an odd, mechanical way that she repeated the question, only to receive the same answer. Then another man, looking in some curious way "like an old picture," ran up behind them, urging them in a strange accent in which they had never heard French spoken before, to go to the left. They followed his instructions, but upon turning around to thank him, Miss Moberly could not see him; she could only hear the sound of his running feet.

Other figures appeared, men with unusually long hair and buckled shoes, a woman and a girl in the doorway of a cottage, both wearing the quaintest dresses with white handkerchiefs tucked into the bodices. The woman was passing a jug to the girl and, as the two English ladies looked at them, their movements were arrested for a moment as in a *tableau vivant*.

At length they came to the Petit Trianon and on the rough grass that grew quite up to the terrace a lady was sitting. She had on a shady white hat "perched on a good deal of fair hair" that fluffed around her forehead. Miss Moberly thought she was a tourist, but her dress was so "old-fashioned and so unusual." The strange-looking lady looked up. It was not a young face, although it was a rather pretty one. "I looked straight at her," Miss Moberly said; "but some indescribable feeling made me turn away."

Miss Moberly had not recognized the lady on the lawn; but later, when endeavoring to understand the experiences of this extraordinary day, she turned over the pages of a book about the Petit Trianon. She came upon a picture by Wertmüller that she immediately knew to be a likeness of the face she had seen: it was a portrait of Marie Antoinette.

VERSAILLES
IN LITERATURE

LADIES AT COURT

The Marquise de Sévigné's letters to her daughter, Mme. de Grignan, are famed for the intimate glimpse they provide of seventeenth-century court life in France and for the remarkable prose style of their author. A well-bred lady of fashion who preferred her country estate to the formality of Louis XIV's court, the marquise described public and private events with a verve and wit that have rarely been equaled.

Paris, Wednesday 29 July.

Here's a change of scene, my dear, which will appeal to you as much as to the rest of the world. I went with the Villars's to Versailles on Saturday. You know the usual court procedure, the Queen's robing, Mass followed by dinner, but it is no longer imperative to stifle whilst Their Majesties are at table, for at three o'clock the magnificent royal suite is thrown open and the King and Queen, MONSIEUR, MADAME and MADEMOISELLE, the princes and princesses, Madame de Montespan and her suite, the courtiers and their ladies, indeed the entire French Court assemble there. The apartments are sumptuously furnished and as there is no crowd to speak of one does not feel the heat unduly, and the guests move from room to room without being crushed to death. A game of *reversi* sets the tone for the evening. The King stands behind Mme de Montespan who holds the cards; MONSIEUR, the Queen and Mme de Soubise also take part; Dangeau and Co.; Langlée and Co.; a thousand louis are flung on the table, no other counters being used. I watched Dangeau [a courtier renowned for his skillful gambling] play and realised what innocents we all were compared with him. He is absorbed in the game to the exclusion of all else; he neglects nothing which can be turned to his own advantage, in a word his good judgement overrides the vagaries of fortune, and two hundred thousand francs in ten days, a hundred thousand *écus* in a month all go on the credit side of his ledger. He drew me into partnership with him, so I was admirably placed. As you instructed me to do, I bowed to the King who bowed back as if I were young and lovely. The Queen talked at length of my illness and cure as if I had lately been through the pangs of childbirth. She also spoke to me of you. M. le Duc lavished his usual meaningless caresses on me . . . . Mme de Montespan spoke to me of Bourbon and asked me to tell her about Vichy, and the benefit I had derived from it, saying that far from curing her knee Bourbon had given her a pain in both. She holds herself as straight as a ramrod, in the words of Maréchale de la Meilleraye, but quite seriously, I find her beauty dazzling; she has lost weight, but this has in no way impaired her complexion, eyes, or lips. Her dress was of French point lace, her head adorned with hundreds of little curls, the two longest hanging down on each side of her face, and a black ribbon threaded through the hair. She wore pearls, the property of Mme la Maréchale de l'Hôpital, enriched with curls and festoons of priceless diamonds, as well as three or four bodkins and no coif; in a word beauty triumphant. She was the cynosure of all eyes, sought out by ambassadors, the admiration of the whole assembly. She has met with criticism on the grounds that she deprived the French people of their King and sovereign; now she has graciously handed him back, and you can scarcely believe what rejoicings there are, nor what beauty and sparkle this has lent to the court. This agreeable confusion, this order in disorder among these great and distinguished persons prevails from three to six of the clock. When a courier is announced the King retires to read his letters, returns anon and is always

PLAN DV
LABIRINTHE
DE VERSAILLES.

One of the small and unexpected delights of Versailles in the time of Louis XIV was a wooded labyrinth in the southeast corner of the gardens. Above are the plan and main entrance, while on the following pages of Versailles in Literature *are some of the fountains, aviaries, and repetitive vistas that must have made getting lost in the bosky maze a lovely, surprising diversion.*

ready to listen to any music being played, which makes a favorable impression. . . . At six the company move off and are shown to their carriages, the King takes his seat with Mme de Montespan at his side, Monsieur, Madame de Thianges and the good d'Heudicourt on the back seat. You know how these *calèches* are made; they do not sit facing each other, but all look the same way. The Queen rides in another with the Princesses, followed by a crowd manoeuvering for places as best they can. Later on the guests are rowed in gondolas on the canal to the strains of music, returning about ten, when a play is staged, and at the stroke of midnight *medianoche* is served; thus Saturday draws to its close.

MARQUISE DE SÉVIGNÉ
Letters, 1676

The voluminous correspondence of Elisabeth Charlotte of Bavaria, known as Madame, is a treasure house of information on Versailles in its heyday. An outsider at court by choice as well as circumstance, Madame compensated for her unhappy marriage to Monsieur — Louis XIV's younger brother — by writing frank and unabashedly biased letters to her numerous German relations. She found fault with everyone and everything at Versailles, with the single exception of the king himself.

14th *December,* 1676, St. Germain.

To *the* Duchess of Hanover.

I beg you to accept my excuses for not having written to you for an eternity. In the first place, I have been to Versailles where we were busy the entire day. From morning until three o'clock in the afternoon we went hunting. On our return from the chase we changed our dresses and went upstairs to the gaming, where we stayed until seven o'clock in the evening. Then we went to the play, which did not end until half-past ten o'clock. After the play came supper, followed by a ball, which usually lasted until three o'clock in the morning, and only then could we go to bed. I leave you to guess whether I had time for letter-writing. Since my return here I have endeavoured each day to reply to your letter, but I have been constantly hindered from doing so, especially by unwelcome visitors, for whom I have to thank a fall from my horse. I must tell you this story. We had already caught a hare and put a magpie to flight, and were going along very slowly, when I observed that my habit was not very elegantly arranged beneath me. I stopped my horse and leant over to adjust it, but while I was still in this position a hare started up and everyone set off in pursuit. My horse, seeing the others start off, wished to follow them, and gave a lurch to the side. I was already half out of the saddle, and this jerk made me quit it almost entirely. I seized the pommel without taking my foot out of the stirrup, hoping thus to regain my balance, but the moment I took hold of the pommel I lost the reins. I shouted to a cavalier who was ahead of me to stop my horse, but he rushed at me with such impetuosity that my horse took fright, and instead of stopping, turned in another direction and bolted. I held on tightly as long as I saw other horses near me, but when I found myself alone I quietly disengaged myself and dropped gently to the green turf. So much fortune had I that, Heaven be praised, I came by not the smallest hurt. You, who so greatly admired the King for the attentions he paid me during my lying-in, will like him all the more in this affair, for he was the first to reach my side. He was as pale as death, and I had to assure him earnestly that I had come to no harm and had not fallen on my head. His anxiety was not relieved until he had himself examined every part of my head. At length, having assured himself that I had told the truth, he conducted me to my apartment, where he remained some time longer to see that I didn't swoon. Indeed, he only returned to the old castle when I had assured him positively that I didn't feel the least bit ill . . . . To tell the truth, I am more in favour with the King every day. He always speaks to me when he meets me, and nowadays he sends for me every Saturday to dine with him in Madame de Montespan's room. That means that I am actually very much the fashion, and that the courtiers admire whatever I say and whatever I do, whether it be good or bad. They carry their admiration to such an extent that when it occurred to me during this very cold weather to put on my old zibeline in order to keep my neck warm, they all had them made to the same pattern, and they are now the height of fashion. I have a good laugh at this, for these folk who now admire this fashion so greatly are precisely those who, five years ago, used to mock at me and my zibeline so much that I dare not put it on. Things happen like that at this court. If the courtiers think you are in favour you may do what you like and you are sure of approval, but if they think the contrary, they would hold you up to ridicule, even if you came straight from Heaven. I wish you could come and spend a few months here and see the sort of life we lead. I am sure that you would be heartily amused.

MADAME
Letters, 1676

Although gala festivities had become commonplace at Versailles by 1697, the wedding celebration of the Duc de Bourgogne — Louis XIV's favorite grandson — and Marie Adélaide was exceptionally grand. From Madame's perspective, however, it was more an occasion for sore feet than glittering splendor.

8th *December,* 1697, Versailles.

To *the* DUCHESS OF HANOVER.

Your kind letter arrived in time yesterday to cheer me up and make me forget the weariness I had to endure during the wedding. There was such a crush that I had to wait a quarter of an hour at each door before I could enter, and my dress and petticoat were so frightfully heavy that I could hardly stand upright. The dress was of gold, covered with raised flowers of black chenil, and my ornaments were pearls and diamonds. Monsieur had a habit of black velvet embroidered in gold, and he wore all his big diamonds; my son's costume was embroidered in gold and various colours, and was completely covered with gems. My daughter wore a gown of green velvet, embroidered in gold; the gown and underskirt were studded all over with rubies and diamonds, and so was the corsage; the embroidery was so exquisitely made that each flower stood out as if it were embossed; her headdress consisted of several *enseignes* made of brilliants, and ruby *poinçons* with a golden ribbon completely covered with diamonds. The King wore a habit of cloth of gold with hair-coloured embroidery on it. Monseigneur also wore a habit of cloth of gold covered with golden embroideries. The bridegroom wore a black mantle worked in gold with a white doublet embroidered in gold with diamond buckles. His mantle was lined with rose and embroidered in gold, silver, and hair-colour.

The bride had a dress of cloth of silver and an underskirt with silver ribbons decorated with rubies and diamonds. All the diamonds she wore in her hair and elsewhere were crown jewels. . . . A quarter of an hour before mid-day we went to Mass, which was only a Low Mass recited by Cardinal de Coislin in his capacity of Chief Almoner. Before the Mass began, the betrothal was celebrated. The King, Monseigneur, Monsieur and I stood round the betrothed couple. When the moment came to say "I will," the bride bowed four times, but the bridegroom only twice, because he had only to ask the consent of his father and grandfather, while the bride asked Monsieur's and mine as well, since we are her grandparents. When the Mass began the King and the rest of us returned to our places, while the betrothed remained kneeling before the altar.

I forgot to say that the ceremony took place in the King's drawing-room. The bridegroom went to fetch his betrothed, led her forward, then they both walked immediately in front of the King. After the Mass was finished, the register was signed by the King, the bride, the bridegroom, and Monsieur and me as relations. Then by the Duc d'Anjou, the Duc de Berri, my son and Monsieur le Prince as witnesses. When we withdrew the bride took her rank as Duchesse de Bourgogne behind the King, but the bridegroom still escorted her. We sat down directly at the table. It was in the shape of a horseshoe, and no one had a place except the members of the Royal Family, and the bastards. Madame de Verneuil was there, too, because she is the widow of the bastard son of Henry IV. I was not dull at the table because I was next to my dear Duc de Berri, who kept me laughing. "I see my brother," he said, "winking at his little wife, but if I liked I could make eyes at her too, because I have known how to ogle for a long time now. You have only to look straight ahead, then sideways." As he said this he imitated his brother so funnily that I could not help laughing at him. After the feast we repaired to the Duchesse de Bourgogne's chamber, and stayed there a quarter of an hour without sitting down. Then everyone separated to their own rooms. At seven o'clock we again assembled in the King's suite. There was such a crush that the King, who had been to visit Madame de Maintenon, could not get through, and had to wait for a quarter of an hour at the door until the crowd had thinned a little. We had to wait three-quarters of an hour in the King's drawing-room for the arrival of the English Royal Family. The King, the bride, and all the rest of us went as far as the antechamber to meet their Majesties. The Queen was dressed in cloth of gold with black flowers and a parure of diamonds. The King wore hair-coloured velvet with diamond buttons. We went in procession to the great hall, where we remained for three-quarters of an hour. From there we went into the gallery to see the display of fireworks. . . .

Immediately after supper the bride was taken to her room and disrobed. The Queen handed her her nightdress, and the King of England did the same for the Duc de Bourgogne. The bride's dressing table was beautifully equipped, and her bedspread was trimmed with lace a foot deep. It was Venetian point lace, but had been made in Paris with the arms of the bridal couple worked in it. As soon as they had finished putting the bridegroom to bed, the King called the ambassador of Savoy, and showed him the two of them in bed. The ambassador immediately dispatched a gentleman to hasten to the Duke of Savoy with the news. After that everyone went home. This morning nothing interesting has happened, but this evening at six o'clock the King will hold a large reception with the Duchesse de Bourgogne until a quarter past seven o'clock, when there will be an *appartement*. We are all wearing full Court dress again to-day.

MADAME
Letters, 1697

DEATH OF THE SUN KING

Despite her acid pen and defiant independence, Madame was genuinely devoted to Louis XIV and grieved bitterly at his deathbed. Her position at court, however, was immensely improved by the king's demise and the appointment of her son, the Duc d'Orléans, as regent of France.

27th *August,* 1715, Versailles.

To *the* RAUGRAVINE LOUISA.

First of all I must tell you that yesterday we saw the most sad and moving sight it would be possible to imagine. The King, after being prepared for death and receiving the last sacrament, sent for the Dauphin to speak to him and give him his blessing. Then he sent for me as well as the Duchesse de Berri and all his other daughters and grandchildren. He bade me farewell so affectionately that I marvel I did not fall down in a swoon. He assured me that he had always loved me even more than I myself imagined, and that he was sorry he had sometimes caused me sorrow. He asked me to think of him sometimes, adding that he knew I would do so gladly because he was sure that I had always been fond of him. He said also that he gave me his blessing and hoped that I would be happy all my life. I threw myself at his feet, took his hand, and kissed it. Then he embraced me and turned to the others. To them he recommended that they should stand by each other. I thought that he was talking to me and replied that in that, as in everything else, I would obey his Majesty as long as I lived. He began to laugh and said, "It is not on your account that I speak thus; I know that you do not need such advice, but I am speaking to the other princesses." You can imagine what a state all this has thrown me into. The King's courage is beyond description. He gives his orders as if it were only a question of going on a journey. He has said good-bye to all his household, and has recommended them to my son, whom he appointed Regent, with so much affection that it touches me to the heart. I believe that I shall be the first member of the royal family to follow the King when he dies. He is still alive but is growing feebler and feebler and there is no hope left. When I say that I shall be the first to follow I am thinking first of my advanced age and then, that as soon as the King is dead they will take the young King to Vincennes and we shall all go to Paris, where the air does not suit me at all. I shall stay there in mourning, deprived of exercise and fresh air, and it seems likely that I shall fall ill. It is not true that Madame de Maintenon is dead. She is in perfect health and remains in the King's room, which she never leaves night or day.

6th *September,* 1715, Versailles.

To *the* RAUGRAVINE LOUISA.

It is a long time since I wrote to you, but I could not help it, I was so overwhelmed and in such inexpressible sorrow. The King died last Sunday at nine o'clock in the morning, so you can imagine that I had many visits to

pay and receive, and that I have received and answered many letters. The day before yesterday and to-day two have come from you, but I am not in a fit state to reply to them because I am terribly upset, both by the death of the King and because I must go to that hateful place, Paris. If I were to pass a whole year there I should fall very ill, so I want to leave it as soon as I can and go to Saint-Cloud. All this worries me dreadfully, but self-pity leads nowhere. It would be better for me to answer your letter. I am very frank and natural and say whatever comes into my head, so I shall tell you that it was a great comfort to me to see all the people and the entire Army and Parliament come to see my son and publicly acknowledge him as Regent. His enemies, who were plotting all around the King's deathbed, have all been frustrated and their followers have had to leave the lists. But my son takes his responsibilities so much to heart that he has no rest night or day, and I am afraid that he may become ill. All sorts of mournful ideas come into my head, but I cannot tell you of them.

MADAME
Letters, 1715

The Duc de Saint-Simon was perhaps the most acute observer of life at Versailles in all its grandeur and pettiness. His candid Memoirs *are filled with deft and often malicious character sketches of Louis XIV and his entourage. Although Saint-Simon spent most of his adult life immersed in the intrigues endemic among courtiers, his repugnance for Versailles itself was intense and unabating. After minutely recording the king's last days, Saint-Simon freely vented his acrimony.*

Louis XIV. was a prince in whom we cannot deny much that was good, even great, while we recognize still more that was petty and bad, without being able to discern what was native in him, and what was acquired. . . .

. . . His buildings, who can count them? And who does not deplore the pride, capriciousness, and bad taste they exhibit? He abandoned the beautiful Saint-Germain, and never did anything for the adornment and convenience of Paris, except (from pure necessity) the Pont Royal, so that Paris, with her incomparable site, is inferior to many cities in various parts of Europe. . . .

Saint-Germain, a spot unique for its collection of delightful views and the immense extent of level forest that adjoins it; unique also for the beauty of its trees, its soil, its situation, the abundance and convenience of its springs of water, the charm of its gardens, its slopes and terraces, and for the beauty and convenience of the Seine; in fact a city ready made, the position of which provided it with everything needful, — all this he abandoned for Versailles, the gloomiest and most thankless of places; without view, without woods, without water, without soil, for all is either sand or bog, consequently with an air that cannot be pure.

He delighted in tyrannizing over nature, in subduing it by force of art and money. He raised buildings one after another on that spot without any general design; the fine and the villanous were huddled together, the vast and the cramped. His apartments and those of the queen are most inconvenient, looking out at the back on privies and other dark, closed-in, and evil-smelling places. The gardens, the magnificence of which amazes, while the slightest use of them is repulsive, are in the worst taste. One can only reach shade by crossing a vast torrid zone, at the end of which there is nothing to do but go up or down a hill, which is very short and ends the gardens. The rubble pavement burns the feet, but without it one would sink in the sand or the mud. The violence everywhere done to nature repels and disgusts the mind. The volumes of water collected and forced in on all sides make these gardens verdant, rank, and miry; they exhale an unhealthy dampness which is very perceptible, and an odour that is more so. Their vistas, which have been carefully managed, are incomparable; but that is all, and the result is that we admire and flee. On the courtyard side, the narrowness is suffocating, and the vast wings of the château spread away without holding to anything. On the garden front, one might enjoy the beauty of the *tout-ensemble*, but the building looks like a half-burned palace with the upper story and the roofs missing. The chapel, which overtops everything because Mansart wanted to oblige the king to put on a whole upper story, presents on all sides the melancholy appearance of a great catafalque. The workmanship of every kind is exquisite; the plan of it *nil;* it is built entirely with regard to the king's pew above, for he never entered the chapel from below. It would be endless to mention the monstrous defects of a palace so immense and so immensely expensive, with its adjuncts that were even more so. This Versailles of Louis XIV., this masterpiece so ruinously dear and in such bad taste, where the mere changes of fountains and groves have buried more money than could ever appear, he never finished. Among all the many salons crowding one upon another there is no banqueting hall, no ballroom, no theatre. Before and behind the palace, much remains to be done. The parks and avenues, newly planted, have still to grow; gutters many leagues in length are still to be made; even the walls, that within their vast contour inclose a little province of the gloomiest and most wretched bit of land in the world, are not wholly finished.

DUC DE SAINT-SIMON
Memoirs, 1715

AMERICANS AT VERSAILLES

Benjamin Franklin, the "Renaissance man" of Colonial America, was sent to England in 1766 to defend Colonial opposition to the Stamp Tax. During the course of his mission — which grew in duration and responsibility as tensions with the mother country increased — Franklin frequently crossed the channel to France. In a letter to the daughter of his English landlady, he described his impressions of the court of Louis XV.

Paris, Sept. 14. 1767

Dear Polly

I am always pleas'd with a Letter from you, and I flatter myself you may be sometimes pleas'd in receiving one from me, tho' it should be of little Importance, such as this, which is to consist of a few occasional Remarks made here and in my Journey hither. . . .

. . . you must know I have been at Court. We went to Versailles last Sunday, and had the Honour of being presented to the King, he spoke to both of us very graciously and chearfully, is a handsome Man, has a very lively Look, and appears younger than he is. In the Evening we were at the *Grand Couvert,* where the Family sup in Publick. . . . The Table . . . was half a Hollow Square, the Service Gold. When either made a Sign for Drink, the Word was given by one of the Waiters, *A boire pour le Roy,* or *A boire pour la Reine,* &c. then two Persons within the Square approach'd, one with Wine the other with Water in Caraffes, each drank a little Glass of what they brought, and then put both the Caraffes with a Glass on a Salver and presented it. Their Distance from each other was such as that other Chairs might have been plac'd between any two of them. An Officer of the Court brought us up thro' the Croud of Spectators, and plac'd Sir John so as to stand between the King and Madame Adelaide, and me between the Queen and Madame Victoire. The King talk'd a good deal to Sir John, asking many Questions about our Royal Family; and did me too the Honour of taking some Notice of me; that's saying enough, for I would not have you think me so much pleas'd with this King and Queen as to have a Whit less Regard than I us'd to have for ours. No Frenchman shall go beyond me in thinking my own King and Queen the very best in the World and the most amiable.

Versailles has had infinite Sums laid out in Building it and Supplying it with Water: Some say the Expence exceeded 80 Millions Sterling. The Range of Building is immense, the Garden Front most magnificent all of hewn Stone, the Number of Statues, Figures, Urns, &c in Marble and Bronze of exquisite Workmanship is beyond Conception. But the Waterworks are out of Repair, and so is great Part of the Front next the Town, looking with its shabby half Brick Walls and broken Windows not much better than the Houses in Durham Yard. There is, in short, both at Versailles and Paris, a prodigious Mixture of Magnificence and Negligence, with every kind of Elegance except that of Cleanliness, and what we call *Tidyness.* Tho' I must do Paris the Justice to say, that in two Points of Cleanliness they exceed us. The Water they drink, tho' from the River, they render as pure as that of the best Spring, by filtring it thro' Cisterns fill'd with Sand; and the Streets by constant Sweeping are fit to walk in tho' there is no pav'd foot Path. Accordingly many well dress'd People are constantly seen walking in them.

BENJAMIN FRANKLIN
Letter, 1767

In 1778 John Adams — later the second President of the United States — was instrumental in securing the defensive alliance with France that proved to be a turning point in the War for Independence. In his Autobiography, *the egalitarian statesman recorded his fascination with the rigid court etiquette maintained at Versailles by Louis XVI and his lovely queen, Marie Antoinette.*

June 7. 1778

Went to Versailles in Company with Mr. Lee, Mr. Izard and his Lady, Mr. Lloyd and his Lady and Mr. Francis, a Gentleman who spoke the English Language very well, having resided many Years in England in some diplomatique Character, and who undertook upon this Occasion to conduct Us. Our Objects were to see the Ceremonies and the Procession of the Knights of the Holy Ghost, or the Chevaliers of the Cordon blue, and in the Evening the public Supper of the Royal Family at the grand Couvert. The Kneelings, the Bows, and the Curtesies of the Knights of the Saint Esprit, the Dresses and Decorations, The King seated on his Throne, his investiture of a new created Knight with the Badges and Ornaments of the Order, and his Majesty's profound and reverential Bow before the Altar as he retired, were Novelties and Curiosities to me, but surprized me much less, than the Patience and Perseverance with which they all kneeled for two hours together upon the hard Marble, of which the Floor of the Chapel was made. The distinction of the blue ribbon, was very dearly purchased at the price of enduring this painful Operation, four times in a Year. The Count De Vergennes [minister of foreign affairs] confessed to me, that he was almost dead, with the pain of it. . . .

The Queen was attended by her Ladies to the Gallery opposite to the Altar, placed in the Center of the Seat, and there left alone. . . .

At nine O Clock in the Evening We went to the grand Couvert, and saw the King, Queen and Royal Family at Supper. Whether Mr. Francis had contrived a plott to gratify the Curiosity of the Spectators, or whether the Royal Family had a fancy to see the raw American at their leisure, or whether they were willing to gratify him with a convenient Seat, in which he might see all the Royal Family and all the Splendors of the Place, I know not. But the Scheme could not have been carried into Execution certainly without the orders of the King. I was selected and summoned indeed from all my Company, and ordered to a Seat close beside the Royal Family. The Seats on both Sides of the Hall, arranged like the Seats in a Theater, were all full of Ladies of the first Rank and Fashion in the Kingdom and there was no room or place for me but in the midst of them. It was not easy to make room for one more Person. However Room was made and I was situated between two Ladies, with Rows and Ranks of Ladies above and below me, and on the right hand and on the left [h]and Ladies only. My Dress was a decent French Dress, becoming the Station I held, but not to be compared with [the] Gold and Diamonds and Embroidery about me. I could neither speak nor understand the Language in a manner to support a Conversation: but I had soon the Satisfaction to find it was a silent Meeting, and that nobody spoke a Word but the Royal Family to each other, and they said very little. The Eyes of all the Assembly were turned upon me, and I felt sufficiently humble and mortified, for I was not a proper Object for the criticisms of such a Company. I [found] myself gazed at, as We in America used to gaze at the Sachems who came to make Speeches to Us in Congress, but I thought it very

hard if I could not command as much Power of face, as one of the Chiefs of the Six Nations, and therefore determined that I would assume a chearful Countenance, enjoy the Scene around me and observe it as cooly as an Astronomer contemplates the Starrs. . . . The King was the Royal Carver for himself and all his Family. His Majesty eat[s] like a King and made a Royal Supper of solid Beef and other Things in Proportion. The Queen took a large spoonful of Soupe, and displayed her fine Person and graceful manners, in alternately looking at the Company in various parts of the Hall, and ordering several kinds of Seasoning to be brought to her, by which she fitted her Supper to her Taste. When this was accomplished, her Majesty exhibited to the admiring Spectators, the magnificent Spectacle of a great Queen swallowing her Royal Supper in a single Spoonful, all at once. This was all performed like perfect Clockwork, not a feature of her face, nor a Motion of any part of her Person, especially her Arm and her hand could be criticised as out of order. A little and but a little Conversation seemed to pass among the Royal Personages of both Sexes, but in so low a voice that nothing could be understood by any of the Audience.

The Officers about the Kings Person brought him many Letters and Papers from time to time, while he was at Table. He looked at these, some of them he read or seemed to read, and returned them to the same Officers who brought them or some others.

These Ceremonies and Shows may be condemned by Philosophy and ridiculed by Commedy, with great reason. Yet the common Sense of Mankind has never adopted the rigid decrees of the former, nor ever sincerely laughed with the latter. . . . Something of the kind every Government and every Religion has and must have: and the Business and Duty of Lawgivers and Philosophers is to endeavour to prevent them from being carried too far.

JOHN ADAMS
Autobiography, 1778

The author of the American Declaration of Independence had little patience with French courtiers and fashionable society — although his position as United States Minister to France in the years 1785–89 necessitated attendance at Versailles. One of the rare accounts of Thomas Jefferson at the court of Louis XVI was written by Thomas Lee Shippen, an enthusiastic and impressionable young American.

Yesterday was the finest day I ever saw, the brightest sun, the clearest air, the most delightful temperature. I improved it by going with my best friend Mr. Jefferson to Versailles. He had made choice of that day to present me to the Court. . . .

The ceremony is rather tedious, but carries through the whole of it so much of novelty to a stranger, and so much of Oriental splendor and magnificence, that it is certainly well worth seeing once. We arrived at Versailles at ½ past ten and were not done bowing until near 2. The carriage drove up to the Count de Montmorin's (successor to Count de Vergennes in the department of *foreign affairs,*) where in a large saloon ornamented with pictures larger than life of the Royal family, stood the introductor and his secretary and several members of the Diplomatic Corps. . . . At 12 we left the Count M.'s and crossed the Court to the Salle des Ambassadeurs where coffee, chocolate and wine were offered to our acceptance. After waiting there long enough to read the papers of the day, we were taken successively into the apartments of the King Queen the Princess Victoire and Adelaide (the King's Aunts,) Monsieur, the Count d'Artois, Madame and the Countess d'Artois and the Princess Elizabeth the King's sister and the Arch Bishop or Ministre Principal of France. These personages have all separate households and distinct portions of the Palace allotted to them, and you may form some judgment of the manner in which they support their rank when you know that between them they expend 36,000,000 of livres a year without including any of the contingent expences of Ministers, their tables &c. All the *departments of State* have each of them a suite of rooms in the Palace. The situation of this superb building is worthy of its grandeur, and both well suited to the Court of a great Nation. Lewis the 14th. seems in this as in all his other works to have consulted nothing but the grandeur and glory which ought to shroud his person and adorn his reign. . . . The business of bowing being over, which any but a Scotchman would have been tired of, I left Mr. Jefferson at the C. de M. and went in search of your old pupil Walker who has retired to Versailles to study the French. I found him in decent apartments and in a kind family. We walked out together chapeau à la main and visited the unrivalled gardens of this enchanting paradise — What walks! What groves! What water works! But you have seen them all — and I must leave it to your memory to recal them to your imagination. . . .

. . . When we were introduced to the King, it was after waiting 5 minutes in his antichamber into which we were brought by his direction being told that he was ready to receive us. How did he do it? He was just pulling on his coat, a servant was tying his hair in which there was no powder, while one of his attendants was arranging his sword belt, and when the file of ambassadors Envoys Ministers &c. in full dress, representatives of monarchs mighty as himself and of Republics more great because more virtuous, were prostrating themselves before him emulous of each other in demonstrating their obsequious adulation, he hitched on his sword and hobbled from one side of the room to the other, spoke 3 words to a few of the ambassadors and 2 to a German Prince who was presented with me, and left the room. I revolted at the insufferable arrogance of the King but I was more mortified at the suppleness and base complaisance of his attendants. I rejoiced that I was not a citizen of such a government, but that I belonged to a Country, and that she would always have a right to my services, where the people respect sincerity and acknowledge no other tyranny than that of Honor.

I observed that although Mr. Jefferson was the plainest man in the room, and the most destitute of ribbands crosses and other insignia of rank that he was most courted and most attended to (even by the Courtiers themselves) of the whole Diplomatic corps — The king is bound up by etiquette to distribute his monosyllables among those of *Ambassadorial* rank — consequently he was an exception. This proved to me that substantial sense, extensive acquirements and unimpeached integrity command even among those who cannot boast of their possession, respect veneration and applause, and that they are preferred by all to empty ornament and unmeaning grandeur, when they give themselves time to weigh the intrinsic properties of each, and coolly to form the result. I observed too in the midst of all their splendor an uneasiness and ennui in their faces which did not bespeak content or happines: and this conspired with every thing I had seen before to convince me that *a certain degree of equality* is essential to human bliss.

Happy above all Countries is our Country where *that equality* is found, without destroying the necessary subordination.

THOMAS LEE SHIPPEN
Letter to his father, 1788

END OF AN ERA

Arthur Young, the most celebrated English traveler of the late eighteenth century and a leading expert on modern farming techniques, found French agriculture sadly outdated during his extensive tour of the countryside in 1787 — only two years before the outbreak of the Revolution. At Versailles Young was astonished by Louis XVI's haphazard enforcement of ceremonial rules.

Breakfasted with [the Duc de Liancourt] at his apartments in the palace, which are annexed to his office of grand master of the wardrobe, one of the principal in the court of France. — Here I found the duke surrounded by a circle of noblemen, among whom was the duke de la Rochefoucauld, well known for his attention to natural history. . . .

The ceremony of the day was, the King's investing the Duke of Berri, son of the count D'Artois, with the cordon blue. The Queen's band was in the chapel where the ceremony was performed, but the musical effect was thin and weak. During the service the King was seated between his two brothers, and seemed by his carriage and inattention to wish himself a hunting. He would certainly have been as well employed, as in hearing afterwards from this throne a feudal oath of chivalry, I suppose, or some such nonsense, administered to a boy of ten years old. Seeing so much pompous folly I imagined it was the dauphin, and asked a lady of fashion near me; at which she laughed in my face, as if I had been guilty of the most egregious idiotism: nothing could be done in a worse manner; for the stifling of her expression only marked it the more. I applied to Mons. de la Rochefoucauld to learn what gross absurdity I had been guilty of so unwittingly; when, forsooth, it was because the dauphin, *as all the world knows in* France, has the cordon blue put around him as soon as he is born. So unpardonable was it for a foreigner to be ignorant of such an important part of French history, as that of giving a babe a blue slobbering bib instead of a white one!

After this ceremony was finished, the King and the knights walked in a sort of procession to a small apartment in which he dined, saluting the Queen as they passed. There appeared to be more ease and familiarity than form in this part of the ceremony; her majesty, who, by the way, is the most beautiful woman I saw to-day, received them with a variety of expression. On some she smiled; to others she talked; a few seemed to have the honour of being more in her intimacy. Her return to some was formal, and to others distant. . . . The ceremony of the King's dining in public is more odd than splendid. The Queen sat by him with a cover before her, but ate nothing; conversing with the duke of Orleans, and the duke of Liancourt, who stood behind her chair. To me it would have been a most uncomfortable meal, and were I a sovereign, I would sweep away three-fourths of these stupid forms; if Kings do not dine like other people, they lose much of the pleasure of life; their station is very well calculated to deprive them of much, and they submit to nonsensical customs, the sole tendency of which is to lessen the remainder. . . .

The palace of Versailles, one of the objects of which report had given me the greatest expectation, is not in the least striking: I view it without emotion: the impression it makes is nothing. What can compensate the want of unity? From whatever point viewed, it appears an assemblage of buildings; a splendid quarter of a town, but not a fine edifice; an objection from which the garden front is not free, though by far the most beautiful. — The great gallery is the finest room I have seen; the other apartments are nothing; but the pictures and statues are well known to be a capital collection. The whole palace, except the chapel, seems to be open to all the world; we pushed through an amazing croud of all sorts of people to see the procession, many of them not very well dressed, whence it appears, that no questions are asked. But the officers at the door of the apartment in which the King dined, made a distinction, and would not permit all to enter promiscuously. . . .

. . . To Trianon, to view the Queen's *Jardin Anglois*. I had a letter to Mons. Richard, which procured admittance. It contains about 100 acres, disposed in the taste of what we read of in books of Chinese gardening, whence it is supposed the English style was taken. There is more of Sir William Chambers here than of Mr. Brown — more effort than nature — and more expence than taste. It is not easy to conceive any thing that art can introduce in a garden that is not here; woods, rocks, lawns, lakes, rivers, islands, cascades, grottos, walks, temples, and even villages. There are parts of the design very pretty, and well executed. The only fault is too much crouding; which has led to another, that of cutting the lawn by too many gravel walks, an error to be seen in almost every garden I have met with in France. But the glory of *La Petite Trianon* is the exotic trees and shrubs. The world has been successfully rifled to decorate it. Here are curious and beautiful ones to please the eye of ignorance; and to exercise the memory of science. Of the buildings, the temple of love is truly elegant.

Again to Versailles. In viewing the king's apartment, which he had not left a quarter of an hour, with those slight traits of disorder that shewed he *lived* in it, it was amusing to see the blackguard figures that were walking uncontrouled about the palace, and even in his bed-chamber; men whose rags betrayed them to be in the last stage of poverty, and I was the only person that stared and wondered how the devil they got there. It is impossible not to like this careless indifference and freedom from suspicion. One loves the master of the house, who would not be hurt or offended at seeing his apartment thus occupied, if he returned suddenly; for if there was danger of this, the intrusion would be prevented. This is certainly a feature of that *good temper* which appears to me so visible every where in France. I desired to see the Queen's apartments, but I could not. Is her majesty in it? No. Why then not see it as well as the king's? *Ma foi, Mons. c'est un autre chose.* Ramble through the gardens, and by the grand canal, with absolute astonishment at the exaggerations of writers and travellers. There is magnificence in the quarter of the orangerie, but no beauty any where; there are some statues good enough to wish them under cover. The extent and breadth of the canal are nothing to the eye; and it is not in such good repair as a farmer's horse-pond. The menagerie is well enough, but nothing great. Let those who desire that the buildings and establishments of Louis XIV. should continue the impression made by the writings of Voltaire, go to the canal of Languedoc, and by no means to Versailles.

ARTHUR YOUNG
Travels, 1792

On October 5, 1789, the unimaginable occurred at Versailles — a mob of angry Parisians occupied the palace that for more than one hundred years had been the seat of government and the symbol of monarchy. A poignant account of the royal family's last days there was written by Madame de La Tour du Pin, a young lady-in-waiting to Marie Antoinette.

The fourth of October there was a shortage of bread at several bakers in Paris and a great deal of tumult. One of these bakers was hung, in spite of the efforts of Monsieur de La Fayette and the National Guard. Nevertheless, at Versailles no one was alarmed. They thought that this revolt was similar to those which had already taken place and that the National Guard, of whose loyalty they felt sure, would be able to control the people. Several messages which came to the King and to the President of the Chambers were so reassuring that the fifth of October, at ten o'clock in the morning, the King set out for the hunt in the wood of Verrières, while I myself, after déjeuner, went to rejoin Mme. de Valence who had come to Versailles. We went for a drive in the garden of Mme. Elisabeth at the end of the Grande Avenue. As we descended from the carriage to traverse the *contre-allée*, we saw a man on horseback pass near us at full gallop. It was the Duc de Maillé, who cried out to us: "Paris is marching here with cannon!" This news greatly frightened us, and we returned at once to Versailles, where the alarm had been given.

. . . My husband hastened to his father [M. de La Tour du Pin, Minister of War], who was already in conference with the other Ministers. The first thing that they did was to send in every direction where they thought the hunt might have led the King, to warn him to return. . . . Messengers were sent out at every moment on the highway to obtain news of what was going on. It was learned that an innumerable mob of men with many women were marching upon Versailles; that after this kind of advance guard came the National Guard of Paris with their cannon, followed by a large troop of individuals marching without order. . . .

Finally, at about three o'clock, the King and his suite arrived at full gallop by the Grande Avenue. This unfortunate Prince, instead of stopping and addressing a kind word to [the] fine Flanders Regiment, before which he passed, and which cried: "Vive le Roi!" did not say a single word to them. He went to shut himself up in his apartment, from which he did not come out. The National Guard of Versailles, which was making its first campaign, commenced to murmur and to declare that it would not fire upon the people of Paris. There were no cannon at Versailles. . . .

. . . my father-in-law and Monsieur de Saint-Priest offered the advice that the King should retire to Rambouillet with his family and await there any propositions which might be made to him by the insurgents of Paris and by the National Assembly. The King at first accepted this plan. At about eight or nine o'clock a company of the Gardes du Corps was ordered to the Cour Royale, which they entered by the gate of the Rue de la Sur-Intendance, now the Rue Gambetta. From here they passed by the Terrasse de l'Orangerie, under the windows of the apartments of Queen Marie-Antoinette, traversed the Little Park and gained, by the Ménagerie, the Grande Route to Saint-Cyr. There was left of this troop at Versailles only sufficient men to relieve the posts in the apartments of the King and Queen. The Suisses and the Cent-Suisses guarded their own posts.

It was at this moment that two or three hundred women, who for an hour had been hovering around the gates, discovered a little door opening upon the Rue du Grand-Commun, which was a prolongation of the Rue de la Chancellerie. This door gave access to a secret staircase which ended under that part of the building where we had our quarters in the Cour des Ministres. Some traitor had probably shown them this entrance. They entered in a crowd, knocking down the Swiss guard posted at the top of the stairway, then spread through the court and gained the quarters of the four Ministers which were located in this part of the building. My husband returned at this moment to bring news to his sister and myself. Very much disturbed to find us in such bad company, he accompanied us into the Château. My sister-in-law had taken the precaution of sending her children to the house of a deputy, one of our friends, who was lodged in the city. Guided by Monsieur de La Tour du Pin, we ascended to the Gallery where we found already gathered a number of persons living in the Château, who had come from their apartments to be nearer the source of news.

During this time the King, still hesitating as to what decision to make, was no longer willing to depart for Rambouillet. He consulted everybody. The Queen, equally undecided, could not make up her mind to this flight by night. My father-in-law went down on his knees to the King to implore him to put himself and his family in a place of security. The Ministers would have remained to treat with the insurgents and the Assembly. But the King, repeating continually, "I do not wish to compromise any one," thus lost a precious period of time. At one time it was thought that he was going to yield, and the order was given to prepare the carriages for departure. For two hours they had been ready waiting in the Grande Écurie. No one seemed to think that the people of Versailles would oppose the departure of the Royal family. This, however, is what happened. The moment that the crowd of people from Paris and Versailles who were assembled on the Place d'Armes saw the gate of the court of the Grande Écurie opened, there was a unanimous cry of fear and fury: "Le roi s'en va!" At the same moment they rushed upon the carriages, cut the harness and led the horses back, so that it was necessary to bring word to the Château that the departure was impossible. My father-in-law and Monsieur de Saint-Priest then offered our carriages, which were hitched up outside the railing of the Orangerie, but the King and Queen rejected this proposition, and every one, discouraged, frightened and fearing the greatest misfortunes, remained in silence and suspense.

In this Gallery, witness of all the splendors of the monarchy since Louis XIV, every one walked up and down without exchanging a word. The Queen remained in her room with Mme. Elisabeth, the sister of Louis XVI, and the wife of the Comte de Provence. The Salon de Jeu, hardly lighted, was full of women who were talking in low tones — some seated on stools and others upon the tables. As for myself, my agitation was so great that I could not remain for a moment in the same place. Every few minutes I went to the *oeil-de-boeuf,* from which one could see those who entered and who came out of the King's apartment, in the hope of encountering my husband or my father-in-law and of learning from them some news. The wait to me seemed intolerable.

Finally at midnight, my husband, who had been in the court for some time, came to announce that Monsieur de La Fayette had arrived before the gate of the Cour des Ministres, with the National Guard of Paris, and requested to speak with the King. He added that a part of this Guard, com-

posed of the former Régiment des Gardes, was manifesting much impatience and that the least delay might lead to trouble and even danger.

The King then said: "Have Monsieur de La Fayette come up." In an instant Monsieur de La Tour du Pin was at the gate, and Monsieur de La Fayette, dismounting from his horse, and so fatigued that he was hardly able to stand upright, ascended to the King's apartment accompanied by seven or eight persons, mostly from his staff. . . .

The King, to whom [his officers] had reported that the most absolute calm reigned at Versailles, which at that moment was really true, dismissed all the persons who were still present in the *oeil-de-boeuf* or in his cabinet. The ushers came to the Gallery to tell the ladies who were still there that the Queen had retired. The doors were closed, the candles extinguished, and my husband escorted us back to the apartment of my aunt, which was situated above the Galerie des Princes, at the top of the south wing of the Château. He did not wish to take us back to our rooms in the Ministry on account of the women who were sleeping in the antechambers and who caused us great disgust. . . .

Day was commencing to break. It was almost six o'clock, and the most profound silence reigned in the court. Monsieur de La Tour du Pin, leaning out of the window, thought he heard the steps of a great crowd of people which seemed to ascend the *rampe* that led to the Cour des Ministres, from the Rue de la Sur-Intendance. Then, to his great surprise, he saw a mob of miserable creatures enter by the gate, although it had been closed and locked. The key had been obtained by an act of treason. The crowd was armed with axes and sabres. . . .

During this time my sister-in-law and I were sleeping in one of the apartments of my aunt, Mme. d'Hénin. My fatigue was so great that my sister-in-law had considerable trouble in awakening me. As neither of us was undressed, we both rushed to the room of my aunt, which looked out upon the park, and where she was unable to hear anything. Her fright was equal to our own. We immediately called our servants. . . .

. . . my husband arrived. He told us that on seeing the assassins penetrate into the Cour Royale, he had immediately rushed to the *grand'garde* stationed upon the Place d'Armes to have the drums beat the alarm. We also learned from him that the Queen had been able to save herself by going to the King's apartment through a little passage, arranged under the room known as the *Œil-de-Bœuf,* which formed the means of communication between her bedroom and that of the King. He persuaded us to leave my aunt's apartment, which was too near, in his opinion, to those of the King and Queen, and counselled us to rejoin Mme. de Simaine, who was lodged near the Orangerie. The Abbé de Damas came to find us and conduct us there.

At the end of two hours, which seemed to me centuries, my husband sent a valet de chambre to inform me that they were leading the King and Queen to Paris, that the Ministers, the Administration and the National Assembly were quitting Versailles, where he himself had the order to remain to save the Château from pillage after the departure of the King. . . .

About three o'clock Mme. d'Hénin returned to look for me and announced that the sad cortège had set out for Paris, the carriage of the King preceded by the heads of the Gardes du Corps, which their assassins were carrying on the ends of their pikes.

In getting into his carriage, Louis XVI had said to Monsieur de La Tour du Pin: "Vous restez maître ici. Tâchez de me sauver mon pauvre Versailles" ["You are in complete charge here. Try to save my poor Versailles."] This injunction was equivalent to an order, which he was firmly resolved to obey. . . .

I left my refuge with my aunt and returned to the Ministry. A frightful solitude then reigned at Versailles. The only noise which was heard in the Château was that of the doors, the blinds and the window-shutters which were being closed for the first time since the reign of Louis XIV. My husband made all arrangements for the defence of the Château, being convinced that as soon as night arrived, the strange and sinister figures which he saw roaming around the streets and the courts would come together to pillage the Château. Alarmed for my safety, in view of the disorder which he foresaw, he insisted that I should leave with my aunt.

MADAME DE LA TOUR DU PIN
Recollections, 1789

The Reign of Terror that followed the execution of Louis XVI and Marie Antoinette in 1793 left its mark on Versailles as well — the palace was stripped of its incomparable furnishings and objets d'art. *An even more ignominious fate had befallen it by 1802 when J. G. Lemaistre, an Englishman, paid a visit.*

Paris, april 13th, 1802.

At Versailles, we drove to Rambrand's, which is esteemed the principal hotel; but finding, on our arrival, that the best rooms were engaged, we changed our plan, and proceeded to *le Petit Trianon* in the park, which, formerly the much loved retreat of Marie Antoinette, has, in the strange metamorphosis things as well as men have experienced in France, become a common inn.

Having ordered dinner to be prepared in a small room, once celebrated as the luxurious *boudoir* of the ill fated queen, we proceeded to view the curiosities of Versailles. The park has lost some trees, and has been neglected. In other respects, it is not much altered. The *orangerie* still retains, unimpaired, all its beauty. We walked through long avenues of orange trees, all of which are in high health and rich foliage. The gardener assured us, that some of those which were of very large dimensions, had been planted in the reign of Francis I.

We next visited the private library of the former kings of France, situate in a separate house in the town. There is nothing very particular in the building; but there were, above the several doors of the library, extremely pretty paintings of the different capitals of Europe. We were here shown a very beautiful collection of illuminated paintings, representing the splendid *fêtes* and *tournaments* given by the magnificent Lewis XIV.

Thence our guide wished to take us to the national manufactory of fire arms, which is carried on with great activity in this town; but having seen many acknowledgedly superior works of the same kind in England, we declined visiting it, and proceeded at once to the palace. This superb building has not suffered at all during the revolution; though, from being neglected and uninhabited, it has contracted a kind of gloom, which forcibly recals the misfortunes of its last possessors, and the uncertainty of human grandeur. The magnificent furniture, which the apartments once contained, has been removed; but the walls are not without ornament, for the palace having been made (probably with the view of preserving it from popular violence) a *musée central,* or *depôt* of the works of art, now possesses several valuable pictures, and a few excellent statues. . . .

We walked through the vast suite of rooms, which, once the seat of gayety, splendour, luxury, and royal magnificence, are now the abode of solitude, and the monument of fallen grandeur.

It is unnecessary to state the many reflections which this spot created. We failed not to visit the apartment which the unfortunate Lewis XVI occupied on the 6th of october, and in which *Marie Antoinette* took refuge. We were also shown the balcony window (now stopped up), where that virtuous and ill fated princess, *madame Elizabeth,* with a magnanimity truly heroic, presented herself, when the queen was called for, and being taken for her, voluntarily subjected herself to all the brutal violence of an irritated mob.

We likewise saw the opera house, built for the wedding of Lewis XVI, when dauphin, and which, during the last reign, was sometimes used as a theatre, and sometimes as a ball room. The apartment is still perfect, but the scenes and decorations have been removed.

On leaving the palace, we visited several *jets d'eau;* but were prevented from viewing the garden as particularly as we could have wished, a violent shower of rain having overtaken us.

The waterworks and pleasure grounds appear to have been much neglected.

We dined at the *Little Trianon,* and slept there. The room, which fell to my share, was that which the unhappy Lewis formerly occupied, and the key of the door had attached to it a label, on which could still be discovered, though half effaced, the words, "appartement du roi." . . .

Before we left Versailles, we visited the garden of *le petit Trianon,* which is rented by our honest landlady, and which may be seen, by paying a small sum for a ticket at the gate. It is kept in tolerable order, and has still strong marks of that good taste, with which it was originally made. It is really, and not nominally, an english garden; and would, even in our happy island, be deemed as prettily laid out, as the smallness of its extent would permit.

The little theatre, built by the queen, situate within the precincts of these grounds, is still in existence, and has suffered no loss, excepting that of the beautiful glasses with which the boxes were once splendidly illuminated. The last object, to which we were led at Versailles, was "le grand Trianon," that favourite spot of Lewis XVI. This elegant building is also unhurt; and the fine marble pillars, which form the entrance, excited all our admiration. The poverty, into which the inhabitants of the town have fallen, in consequence of the revolution, is strikingly apparent. In every corner, we were surrounded by half-starved and half-naked beggars, whose importunities were not a little troublesome.

J. G. LEMAISTRE
A Rough Sketch of Modern Paris, 1802

TWO LITERARY VIEWS

Although extensive renovations sponsored by Louis Philippe in the 1830's had transformed the long-abandoned château into a museum and picture gallery, English novelist William Makepeace Thackeray found that the spirit of Louis XIV continued to inhabit Versailles.

The town [of Versailles] is, certainly, the most moral of towns. You pass from the railroad station through a long, lonely suburb, with dusty rows of stunted trees on either side, and some few miserable beggars, idle boys, and ragged old women under them. Behind the trees are gaunt, mouldy houses; palaces once, where (in the days of the unbought grace of life) the cheap defence of nations gambled, ogled, swindled, intrigued; whence high-born duchesses used to issue, in old times, to act as chambermaids to lovely Du Barri: and mighty princes rolled away, in gilt caroches, hot for the honor of lighting his Majesty to bed, or of presenting his stockings when he rose, or of holding his napkin when he dined. Tailors, chandlers, tinmen, wretched hucksters, and greengrocers, are now established in the mansions of the old peers; small children are yelling at the doors, with mouths besmeared with bread and treacle; damp rags are hanging out of every one of the windows, steaming in the sun; oyster-shells, cabbage-stalks, broken crockery, old papers, lie basking in the same cheerful light. A solitary water-cart goes jingling down the wide pavement, and spirits a feeble refreshment over the dusty, thirsty stones.

After pacing for some time through such dismal streets, we *deboucher* on the *grande place;* and before us lies the palace dedicated to all the glories of France. In the midst of the great lonely plain this famous residence of King Louis looks low and mean. — Honored pile! Time was when tall musketeers and gilded body-guards allowed none to pass the gate. Fifty years ago, ten thousand drunken women from Paris broke through the charm; and now a tattered commissioner will conduct you through it for a penny, and lead you up to the sacred entrance of the palace.

We will not examine all the glories of France, as here they are portrayed in pictures and marble: catalogues are written about these miles of canvas, representing all the revolutionary battles, from Valmy to Waterloo, — all the triumphs of Louis XIV. — all the mistresses of his successor — and all the great men who have flourished since the French empire began. Military heroes are most of these — fierce constables in shining steel, marshals in voluminous wigs, and brave grenadiers in bearskin caps; some dozens of whom gained crowns, principalities, dukedoms; some hundreds, plunder and epaulets; some millions, death in African sands, or in icy Russian plains, under the guidance, and for the good, of that arch-hero, Napoleon. By far the greater part of "all the glories" of France (as of most other countries) is made up of these military men: and a fine satire it is on the cowardice of mankind, that they pay such an extraordinary homage to the virtue called courage; filling their history-books with tales about it, and nothing but it.

Let them disguise the place, however, as they will, and plaster the walls with bad pictures as they please, it will be hard to think of any family but one, as one traverses this vast gloomy edifice. It has not been humbled to the ground, as a certain palace of Babel was of yore; but it is a monument of fallen pride, not less awful, and would afford matter for a whole library of sermons. The cheap defence of nations expended a thousand millions in the erection of this magnificent dwelling-place. Armies were employed, in the intervals of their warlike labors, to level hills, or pile them up; to turn rivers, and to build aqueducts, and transplant woods, and construct smooth terraces, and long canals. A vast garden grew up in a wilderness, and a stupendous palace in the garden, and a stately city round the palace: the city was peopled with parasites, who daily came to do worship before the creator of these wonders — the Great King. "Dieu seul est grand," ["God alone is great"] said courtly Massillon; but next to him, as the prelate thought, was certainly Louis, his viceregent here upon earth — God's lieutenant-governor of the world, — before whom courtiers used to fall on their knees, and shade their eyes, as if the light of his countenance, like the sun, which shone supreme in heaven, the type of him, was too dazzling to bear.

Did ever the sun shine upon such a king before, in such a palace? — or, rather, did such a king ever shine upon the sun? When Majesty came out of his chamber, in the midst of his superhuman splendors, viz. in his cinnamon-colored coat, embroidered with diamonds; his pyramid of a wig; his red-heeled shoes, that lifted him four inches from the ground, "that he scarcely seemed to touch;" when he came out, blazing upon the dukes and duchesses that waited his rising, — what could the latter do, but cover their eyes, and wink, and tremble? And did he not himself believe, as he stood there, on his high heels, under his ambrosial periwig, that there was something in him more than man — something above Fate?

This, doubtless, was he fain to believe; and if, on very fine days, from his terrace before his gloomy palace of Saint Germains, he could catch a glimpse, in the distance, of a certain white spire of St. Denis, where his race lay buried, he would say to his courtiers, with a sublime condescension, "Gentlemen, you must remember that I, too, am mortal." Surely the lords in waiting could hardly think him serious, and vowed that his Majesty always loved a joke. However, mortal or not, the sight of that sharp spire wounded his Majesty's eyes; and is said, by the legend, to have caused the building of the palace of Babel-Versailles.

WILLIAM MAKEPEACE THACKERAY
The Paris Sketch Book, 1840

Samuel Langhorne Clemens — better known by his nom de plume, Mark Twain — was scornfully unimpressed by nearly every monument he visited during his tour of Europe in 1869. Surprisingly, America's peerless humorist was enchanted by Versailles — if appalled by its cost.

Versailles! It is wonderfully beautiful! You gaze, and stare, and try to understand that it is real, that it is on the earth, that it is not the Garden of Eden — but your brain grows giddy, stupefied by the world of beauty around you, and you half believe you are the dupe of an exquisite dream. The scene thrills one like military music! A noble palace, stretching its ornamented front block upon block away, till it seemed that it would never end; a grand promenade before it, whereon the armies of an empire might parade; all about it rainbows of flowers, and colossal statues that were almost numberless, and yet seemed only scattered over the ample space; broad flights of stone steps leading down from the promenade to lower grounds of the park — stairways that whole regiments might stand to arms upon and have room to spare; vast fountains whose great bronze effigies discharged rivers of sparkling water into the air and mingled a hundred curving jets together in forms of matchless beauty; wide grass-carpeted avenues that branched hither and thither in every direction and wandered to seemingly interminable distances, walled all the way on either side with compact ranks of leafy trees whose branches met above and formed arches as faultless and as symmetrical as ever were carved in stone; and here and there were glimpses of sylvan lakes with miniature ships glassed in their surfaces. And every where — on the palace steps, and the great promenade, around the fountains, among the trees, and far under the arches of the endless avenues, hundreds and hundreds of people in gay costumes walked or ran or danced, and gave to the fairy picture the life and animation which was all of perfection it could have lacked.

It was worth a pilgrimage to see. Every thing is on so gigantic a scale. Nothing is small — nothing is cheap. The statues are all large; the palace is grand; the park covers a fair-sized county; the avenues are interminable. All the distances and all the dimensions about Versailles are vast. I used to think the pictures exaggerated these distances and these dimensions beyond all reason, and that they made Versailles more beautiful than it was possible for any place in the world to be. I know now that the pictures never came up to the subject in any respect, and that no painter could represent Versailles on canvas as beautiful as it is in reality. I used to abuse Louis XIV. for spending two hundred millions of dollars in creating this marvelous park, when bread was so scarce with some of his subjects; but I have forgiven him now. He took a tract of land sixty miles in circumference and set to work to make this park and build this palace and a road to it from Paris. He kept 36,000 men employed daily on it, and the labor was so unhealthy that they used to die and be hauled off by cart-loads every night. The wife of a nobleman of the time speaks of this as an *"inconvenience,"* but naively remarks that "it does not seem worthy of attention in the happy state of tranquillity we now enjoy."

I always thought ill of people at home, who trimmed their shrubbery into pyramids, and squares, and spires, and all manner of unnatural shapes, and when I saw the same thing being practiced in this great park I began to feel dissatisfied. But I soon saw the idea of the thing and the wisdom of it. They

seek the *general* effect. We distort a dozen sickly trees into unaccustomed shapes in a little yard no bigger than a dining-room, and then surely they look absurd enough. But here they take two hundred thousand tall forest trees and set them in a double row; allow no sign of leaf or branch to grow on the trunk lower down than six feet above the ground; from that point the boughs begin to project, and very gradually they extend outward further and further till they meet overhead, and a faultless tunnel of foliage is formed. The arch is mathematically precise. The effect is then very fine. They make trees take fifty different shapes, and so these quaint effects are infinitely varied and picturesque. The trees in no two avenues are shaped alike, and consequently the eye is not fatigued with any thing in the nature of monotonous uniformity. I will drop this subject now, leaving it to others to determine how these people manage to make endless ranks of lofty forest trees grow to just a certain thickness of trunk (say a foot and two-thirds;) how they make them spring to precisely the same height for miles; how they make them grow so close together; how they compel one huge limb to spring from the same identical spot on each tree and form the main sweep of the arch; and how all these things are kept exactly in the same condition, and in the same exquisite shapeliness and symmetry month after month and year after year — for I have tried to reason out the problem, and have failed.

We walked through the great hall of sculpture and the one hundred and fifty galleries of paintings in the palace of Versailles, and felt that to be in such a place was useless unless one had a whole year at his disposal. These pictures are all battle-scenes, and only one solitary little canvas among them all treats of anything but great French victories. We wandered, also, through the Grand Trianon and the Petit Trianon, those monuments of royal prodigality, and with histories so mournful — filled, as it is, with souvenirs of Napoleon the First, and three dead Kings and as many Queens. In one sumptuous bed they had all slept in succession, but no one occupies it now. . . . In a room of the Petit Trianon stood the furniture, just as poor Marie Antoinette left it when the mob came and dragged her and the King to Paris, never to return. Near at hand, in the stables, were prodigious carriages that showed no color but gold — carriages used by former Kings of France on state occasions, and never used now save when a kingly head is to be crowned, or an imperial infant christened. And with them were some curious sleighs, whose bodies were shaped like lions, swans, tigers, etc. — vehicles that had once been handsome with pictured designs and fine work-manship but were dusty and decaying now. They had their history. When Louis XIV. had finished the Grand Trianon, he told Maintenon he had created a Paradise for her, and asked if she could think of any thing now to wish for. He said he wished the Trianon to be perfection — nothing less. She said she could think of but one thing — it was summer, and it was balmy France — yet she would like well to sleigh-ride in the leafy avenues of Versailles! The next morning found miles and miles of grassy avenues spread thick with snowy salt and sugar, and a procession of those quaint sleighs waiting to receive the chief concubine of the gayest and most unprincipled court that France has ever seen!

From sumptuous Versailles, with its palaces, its statues, its gardens and its fountains, we journeyed back to Paris.

SAMUEL LANGHORNE CLEMENS
The Innocents Abroad, 1869

Pierre de Nolhac, curator of Versailles from 1892 to 1920, is credited with almost single-handedly inspiring a renewed appreciation of the château in the twentieth century. The painstaking task of reviving Versailles' former splendor, initiated by Nolhac, continues to this day.

The seventeenth century, which endowed Paris and the provinces with such noble monuments — so greatly honoured to-day — seems to be epitomised in the dwelling of Louis XIV. All the great artists who were his contemporaries collaborated in this work, which aimed at the glorification of the national monarchy. Side by side with Le Brun, or under his orders, worked architects, sculptors, painters, smelters, carvers, and decorators of all kinds, of whom some had genius, but who, considering the influence under which they worked, might have done very well with mere technical skill. The Palace and its gardens are full of their masterpieces. We may regret that the academical school, in which the inspiration of our artists became congealed later on, should have drawn some of the elements of its aesthetic principles from Versailles; but it would be more just to ask ourselves what would be lacking to the self-expression of the French race, and to its legacy of national art, if Versailles had disappeared.

An attentive study of the different parts of Versailles will bring to light, beneath that appearance of unity that is revealed at the first glance, many variations of the style of the seventeenth century. . . .

The real interest of modern Versailles, as it appears to us at the beginning of the twentieth century, is concerned with the decorative art of France, of which we see here some of the most important examples; and also with the history of France, thanks to the Museum of portraits and scenes in the history of the nation, by means of which the life of the past is renewed. Nothing can be more interesting than to discover, on the walls of Louis XIV.'s great apartments, the pictures of the time, representing his Court and his military campaigns; or to find collected in Madame de Maintenon's rooms the portraits of the famous men and women of her day; or to see, in the rooms of the Dauphin, Louis XV.'s son, surrounded by contemporary decorations, the whole of the society of the eighteenth century made to live again for us on canvas. This is a very fruitful study, and several days should be devoted to it.

Versailles, even half-furnished and bare — nay, even mutilated — is nevertheless a splendid page of history, always open before the eyes of the nation, and comprehensible to every one. But, whatever we may do to it, it still remains a huge ruin, and a huge tomb. Its animating principle exists no longer, and will never return to it in any other form; and the magnificence that was admired by two centuries is only to be found in isolated parts. Any effort to reproduce it, by restorations of a too detailed description, are condemned beforehand to failure. Who could pretend to reconstruct nowadays (except by thought and study) the sumptuous effects of the days of the Monarchy? The chimerical hope of restoring the past condition of a monument leads, in most cases, to its complete destruction. Let us rather enjoy what has survived; let us at all costs preserve everything that the touch of time has helped to beautify; let us respect the harmonious whole that it has created; and let us, by the help of the remains that are left, guess what the achievement of Louis XIV. must have been in its magnificent completeness.

PIERRE DE NOLHAC
Versailles and the Trianons, 1906

REFERENCE

Chronology of French History

Entries in boldface refer to Versailles.

1594	Coronation of Henry IV, first Bourbon king
1598	Edict of Nantes issued
1610	Accession of Louis XIII
1624	**Louis XIII builds hunting lodge at Versailles**
1624–42	Administration of Cardinal Richelieu
1631–34	**Versailles enlarged by Philibert Le Roy**
1631–48	French participation in the Thirty Years' War
1643	Five-year-old Louis XIV ascends throne
1648–53	Revolt of the Fronde
1651	**Louis XIV pays first visit to Versailles**
1659	Marriage of Louis XIV and Marie Thérèse of Spain
1661	Louis XIV assumes personal rule upon death of Cardinal Mazarin; birth of the dauphin, later known as Monseigneur; **Louis decides to enlarge the palace at Versailles**
1662–83	Administration of Jean Baptiste Colbert, controller general of finances and special adviser to the king
1664	**First fete held at Versailles; first performance of Molière's *Tartuffe***
1666	Death of Queen Mother Anne; Louise de La Vallière officially recognized as the king's mistress
1668	**Treaty of Aix-la-Chapelle celebrated in a great fete; Louis accepts designs of Louis Le Vau for major enlargement of Versailles**
1669–70	**Construction of the Trianon de Porcelaine on the grounds of Versailles for the king's new mistress, the Marquise de Montespan**
1676	**Jules Hardouin-Mansart begins château at Clagny for Mme. de Montespan; Versailles essentially completed and suitable for prolonged visits by the court**
1678	**Mansart makes further additions and begins Galerie des Glaces;** annexation of Franche-Comté as a result of Treaty of Nimeguen
1679	**Château at Marly begun**
1680	Affair of the Poisons
1682	**Installation of court at Versailles; Louis declares Versailles the seat of government**
1683	Death of Colbert and Queen Marie Thérèse
1685	**Louis marries Mme. de Maintenon secretly; in-**auguration of the Galerie des Glaces; revocation of the Edict of Nantes
1686	League of Augsburg formed against France
1687	**Demolition of the Trianon de Porcelaine; Mansart and Robert de Cotte begin work on Trianon de Marbre**
1688	**Trianon de Marbre completed**
1689	**Silver plate melted down to help pay for war of the League of Augsburg**
1690	Death of the dauphine, Monseigneur's wife
1691	Mme. de Montespan retires from court
1695	Order of Saint Louis created
1697	**Marriage of Duc de Bourgogne, Louis's eldest grandson, to Marie Adélaïde;** Treaty of Ryswick
1699	**Major expansions at Marly; work begun on chapel**
1700	Louis announces that the Duc d'Anjou, his grandson, has been named **King of Spain (Philip V)**
1701–13	War of the Spanish Succession
1702	**Major redecorations undertaken;** death of Monsieur, Louis's brother
1707	Death of Mme. de Montespan
1709	Severe winter leads to insurrections in Paris
1710	**Completed chapel consecrated by Cardinal de Noailles**
1711	Death of the dauphin (Monseigneur)
1712	**Deaths of the Duc and Duchesse de Bourgogne**
1713	Treaty of Utrecht confirms permanent separation of crowns of France and Spain
1715	**Death of Louis XIV at Versailles;** accession of Louis XV; Duc d'Orléans named regent
1717	**Peter the Great visits Versailles**
1718–20	War with Spain
1722	**Court returns after seven-year absence**
1725	Louis XV marries Maria Leszczynska of Poland
1736	**Salon d'Hercule completed**
1740–48	War of the Austrian Succession
1741	**Louis XV gives Trianon to the queen**
1745	**Marquise de Pompadour becomes Louis XV's mistress; ball held for marriage of the dauphin**
1748	**Salle de Spectacle (Opéra), designed by Gabriel,**

	begun; the Hermitage built for Mme. de Pompadour
1756–63	Seven Years' War
1757	**King stabbed by would-be assassin at Versailles**
1762	**Petit Trianon begun for Mme. de Pompadour**
1764	**Death of Mme. de Pompadour at Versailles**
1768	**Death of Queen Maria; Comtesse du Barry, presented at court, becomes king's mistress**
1770	**Salle de Spectacle completed; Petit Trianon completed; Marie Antoinette marries the dauphin, Louis XV's grandson, at Versailles**
1774	**Death of Louis XV at Versailles; accession of Louis XVI, who gives Petit Trianon to his queen**
1777	**Marie Antoinette's brother, Emperor Joseph II, arrives at Versailles incognito**
1778–83	French participation in the War for American Independence
1781	**Birth of the dauphin**
1783	**The Hameau, a miniature village, laid out at the Petit Trianon for Marie Antoinette**
1784	**Fete given in honor of Gustavus III of Sweden**
1785	The Affair of the Necklace
1789	**Meeting of the Estates-General at Versailles; death of the dauphin; storming of the Bastille; declaration of the Rights of Man proclaimed; mobs march on Versailles and escort royal family to Paris**
1792	Abolition of the monarchy
1793	Execution of Louis XVI and his wife; beginning of the Reign of Terror; **sale of effects and furnishings from Versailles**
1804	Napoleon crowned emperor
1809	**Napoleon spends week at Versailles following his divorce from Joséphine**
1814	Restoration of the monarchy; **Louis XVIII returns to Versailles for a brief visit**
1815	Battle of Waterloo
1817–20	**Minor repairs made**
1818	**Louis XVIII entertains Duke of Wellington**
1819	**Louis XVIII rejects plan to return the court to Versailles**
1820	**Chapel, restored by Louis XVIII, reconsecrated**
1824	Death of Louis XVIII; accession of Charles X
1826	**Charles X pays first and only visit to Versailles**
1830	July Revolution; Louis Philippe elected king
1833–37	**Versailles transformed into a museum**
1848	**Abdication of Louis Philippe; Louis Napoleon, proclaimed president of the new republic, undertakes massive restoration of Versailles**
1852	Coronation of Louis Napoleon as Napoleon III
1856	**Napoleon III entertains Queen Victoria at Versailles**
1870–71	**Franco-Prussian War; German soldiers billeted at Versailles; Napoleon III capitulates; Third Republic proclaimed; Paris Commune defeated by government troops**
1871	**Wilhelm I proclaimed emperor of a united Germany in Galerie des Glaces; Republican government installed at Versailles**
1879	Seat of government returned to Paris
1892–1920	**Pierre de Nolhac, new curator, sponsors extensive restoration and reconstruction of Versailles museum**
1894–1906	The Dreyfus Affair
1896	**Tsar Nicholas II of Russia visits Versailles**
1905	Official separation of Church and State
1914–18	World War I
1919	**Treaty of Versailles ending World War I signed in Galerie des Glaces**
1925–26	**Large grant made by John D. Rockefeller, Jr. to the French government for restoration of historic buildings, including Versailles**
1939–45	World War II
1940	German forces occupy Paris; fall of France
1944	Liberation of Paris
1945–46	Charles de Gaulle serves as interim president
1954	**Grant by Rockefeller Brothers Fund for further renovation of Versailles**
1957	France joins the European Economic Community
1958–59	De Gaulle — recalled during crisis over Algeria — named premier, then president of the Fifth Republic
1969	De Gaulle resigns; Pompidou elected president
1970	Funeral for Charles de Gaulle

Royal Houses of France: 1589-1848

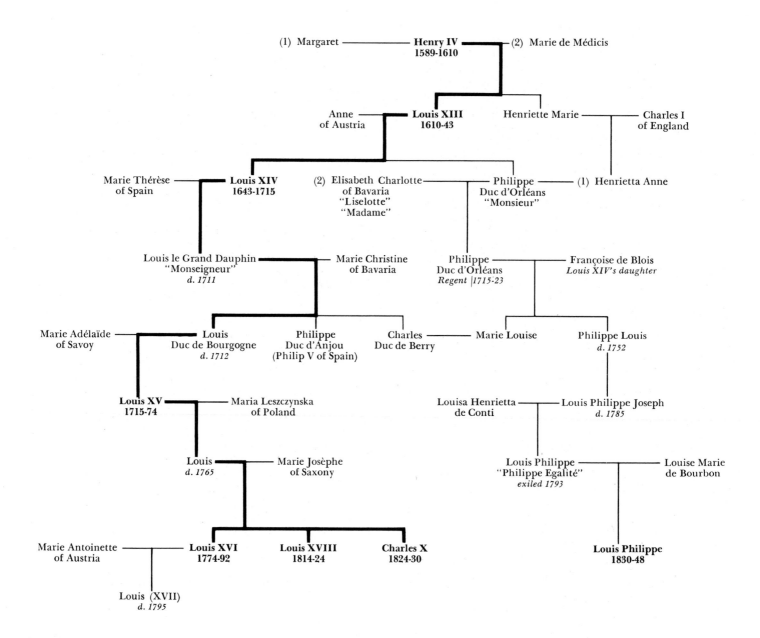

(1) Margaret ——— **Henry IV**
1589-1610 ——— (2) Marie de Médicis

Anne ——— **Louis XIII**
of Austria ——— **1610-43**   Henriette Marie ——— Charles I
of England

Marie Thérèse ——— **Louis XIV**
of Spain   **1643-1715**   (2) Elisabeth Charlotte
of Bavaria
"Liselotte"
"Madame" ——— Philippe
Duc d'Orléans
"Monsieur" ——— (1) Henrietta Anne

Louis le Grand Dauphin
"Monseigneur"
d. 1711 ——— Marie Christine
of Bavaria   Philippe
Duc d'Orléans
Regent |1715-23 ——— Françoise de Blois
Louis XIV's daughter

Marie Adélaïde
of Savoy ——— Louis
Duc de Bourgogne
d. 1712   Philippe
Duc d'Anjou
(Philip V of Spain)   Charles
Duc de Berry ——— Marie Louise   Philippe Louis
d. 1752

Louis XV
1715-74 ——— Maria Leszczynska
of Poland   Louisa Henrietta ——— Louis Philippe Joseph
de Conti   *d. 1785*

Louis
d. 1765 ——— Marie Josèphe
of Saxony   Louis Philippe
"Philippe Egalité"
exiled 1793 ——— Louise Marie
de Bourbon

Marie Antoinette ——— **Louis XVI**
of Austria   **1774-92**   **Louis XVIII**
1814-24   **Charles X**
1824-30   **Louis Philippe**
1830-48

Louis (XVII)
d. 1795

Guide to the Châteaux of France

The majestic châteaux scattered throughout the French countryside are architectural mementos of a glorious past. For centuries the wealthy and the well-born built their palatial country estates on vast plots of choice land; today, through the vicissitudes of revolution and fortune, many are unoccupied, stripped of much of their original furnishings, and transformed into public museums. Others remain in private hands, painstakingly restored and maintained by their successive owners.

Unfortunately, any brief guide to the châteaux must necessarily omit many that are worthy of inclusion either for their excellence of construction or for their wealth of historical associations. The most famous châteaux are in the lush Loire Valley in central France. Known as the "garden of France," the region encompasses the districts of Anjou, Touraine, Blois, and Orléans. Four major rivers water the valley — the Cher, Indre, Vienne, and Loire itself.

The château of **Blois,** begun in the thirteenth century by the Chatillon family, became one of the chief residences of the Renaissance kings of France. In the early fifteenth century it was purchased by Louis, Duc d'Orléans, whose son Charles demolished part of the old fortress and added a small, elegant gallery. By the time Charles's son, the future King Louis XII, was born, Blois had become a literary and artistic center.

With the accession of Louis XII in 1498, the château became the unofficial seat of government and the favorite home of the king and his wife, Anne of Brittany. Louis built a chapel in the house and a small stone and brick wing.

His son, Francis I, renovated the structure, adding a northern wing with a flamboyant Italianate façade and an upper gallery over two stories of loges. The most outstanding feature of this new wing was its huge open-framework spiral staircase set in an octagonal well.

During the reign of Henry III the Estates-General met twice at Blois. In 1588 five hundred deputies, most of them supporters of the powerful Duc de Guise — who hoped to overthrow the king — assembled at the château. Henry foiled the plot by having his rival murdered in a room on the second floor.

In 1617 Louis XIII sent his mother, Marie de Médicis, into exile at Blois but within two years she managed to escape by means of a rope ladder into the moat. In 1626 the king presented the château to his brother Gaston d'Orléans, who

commissioned François Mansart to rebuild the structure. Only the western wing — two pavilions set at right angles — was completed.

After the accession of Louis XIV in 1643 Blois ceased to be a royal residence. By the mid-eighteenth century it had fallen into disrepair. Restored to its former elegance, Blois today houses a museum of painting, sculpture, and religious art.

The château of **Chenonceaux,** on the banks of the Cher, has perhaps the most picturesque site of all the country houses in the Loire Valley. It is known as the "castle of six women" because its history has been intimately associated with females.

During the reign of Francis I, Thomas Bohier, controller of finances for Normandy, purchased the property and demolished its medieval fortress. Between 1515 and 1522 his wife, Catherine Briçonnet, supervised the construction of the present rectangular manor house, with its four corbelled turrets. After Bohier's death the château passed into the royal domain.

In 1547 Henry II presented Chenonceaux to his beautiful mistress, Diane of Poitiers. During her residence there, Philibert Delorme constructed a five-span bridge linking the structure to the riverbank. Upon Henry's death in 1559, Diane's position was no longer secure — and the king's widow, Catherine de Médicis, compelled her to exchange her beloved Chenonceaux for the nearby château of Chaumont.

On her new property, Catherine added a huge park and several outbuildings, and commissioned Jean Bullant to build a two-story gallery on the bridge. The Queen Mother bequeathed the château to her daughter-in-law, Louise of Lorraine, who retired there following the assassination of her husband, Henry III, in 1589.

In the mid-nineteenth century the Baroness Dupin, wife of a wealthy financier, held a fashionable salon at Chenonceaux. Jean Jacques Rousseau spent a season there, tutoring her son in music. Mme. Dupin's popularity among the local villagers saved the château from the mutilation and vandalism that befell so many others during the Revolution. In 1864 the property was purchased by Mme. Pelouze, who restored it to its original appearance; today it is owned by the Menier family.

The château of **Chaumont,** which Catherine de Médicis forced upon Diane of Poitiers, is set on a hillside plateau overlooking the Loire Valley. The original castle had been demolished and rebuilt on a quadrilateral plan between 1465 and 1510 by the counts of Amboise. In the eighteenth century the northern wing was torn down so that the former inner façades could command a

breathtaking view of the countryside. The fortress-like appearance of the château, with its four wide towers and drawbridge, is softened by the delicate ornamentation of the façades. Today the structure is a museum with a fine collection of Renaissance furniture.

The château of **Chambord,** one of the

most famous in the world, was built by Francis I as his personal retreat. Set in the midst of the forest of Boulogne, three miles from the Loire, the estate is bounded by a twenty-mile wall — the longest in France — that encloses the 13,600-acre park.

The château was completed in 1556. It has a traditional rectangular plan; the central keep, with four circular towers, is flanked by two wings. Its stout walls are pierced by large windows. The most compelling feature of the exterior is the exuberantly decorated roof — with its 365 chimneys, 800 capitals, and a multitude of sculptural details. From the terrace, eighty feet above the ground, Francis and his court watched the hunts that took place on the huge game reserve on the grounds.

In 1669–70 Louis XIV held court at Chambord several times; on one occasion, Molière presented the first performance of *Le Bourgeois Gentilhomme.* Louis XV gave the château to his father-in-law, the deposed Polish king Stanislas; Louis XVI gave it to the Polignac family, who established a stud farm on the estate; today, it belongs to the French government and is open to the public.

The second largest concentration of châteaux is in the Île-de-France, the region around Paris. **Chantilly,** twenty-five miles north of the capital, is near

the bank of the Oise river. In 1560, Jean Bullant built the "little château" on an island on the property for Anne de Montmorency. In the next century Jules Hardouin-Mansart, grand-nephew of the architect of Blois, designed the "great château" for the Condé family. Only the "little château" and the gardens laid out

by André Lenôtre survived the Revolution of 1789.

The Duc de Bourbon, who became regent after the death of Philippe, Duc d'Orléans, in 1723, built the finest stables in the world on the estate. Of pale yellow stone, the magnificent stables once accommodated 240 horses, 140 deer and boar hounds, and countless rooms for grooms, coachmen, huntsmen, etc. Between 1876 and 1882 the Duc d'Aumale, the son of Louis Philippe, built a new "great château" to house his 40,000-volume library. Today, Chantilly also houses more than six hundred canvases, including works by Clouet, Raphael, Poussin, Watteau, Ingres, and Delacroix.

The château of **Rambouillet** is the official summer residence of the president of the republic. It was purchased in 1706 by Louis XIV for his son the Count of Toulouse. The count enlarged the château — which had been constructed over the course of several centuries — and installed the exquisite interior paneling.

The gardens and canals of Rambouillet are patterned after those of Lenôtre. On the grounds are a dairy and a shell-covered pavilion that was built by Louis XVI for Marie Antoinette. Both have

been restored and contain much of their original furnishings.

The charming château of **Maintenon,** between Rambouillet and Chartres, was built during the Middle Ages. In 1509 Jean Cottereau, treasurer to Louis XII, purchased the property. In the seventeenth century Louis XIV presented it to his mistress, Mme. de Maintenon. No expense was spared in making the estate suitable for royal visits — Mansart carried out the alterations on the structure itself and Lenôtre planned the elaborate gardens. On the grounds are the ruins of the abandoned aqueduct by Vauban that was to have diverted the waters of the Eure to Versailles.

One of the most popular royal residences was the château of **Fontaine-bleau,** thirty-eight miles south of Paris. Many of the kings of France altered the property to suit their tastes. The original fifteenth-century structure was first embellished by Henry II and Henry IV. During the reign of Francis I the oval

court and striking inner façades were constructed. Louis XIII was responsible for the unusual horseshoe-shaped staircase; Louis XV built a vast house in the gardens. Although the interior was gutted during the Revolution, Napoleon — who preferred the château to Versailles — completely refurbished it.

The original château of **Saint-Germain,** built in the twelfth century by Louis VI, was destroyed early in the Hundred Years' War and rebuilt by Charles V. The present château was designed in 1515 by Pierre Chambiges for Francis I. An irregular pentagon in form, its flat roof was a novelty at the time. Henry II disliked the château and commissioned a second one on the edge of the nearby plateau. It was completed by Henry IV. Until the time of Louis XIV the two châteaux were the favorite pleasure resort of the monarchy.

Although Louis XIV preferred Versailles to Saint-Germain, he was responsible for the magnificent park that surrounds the château. Lenôtre's grand terrace, 2,500 yards long and lined with ancient lime trees, was finally completed in 1673.

By 1776 the château begun by Henry II was in ruins and Louis XVI presented it to his brother, the future Charles X, who demolished most of it. During the reign of Louis Philippe, Saint-Germain was converted into a military prison. Napoleon III restored it and established a museum of national antiquities.

The greatest architectural talents of the seventeenth century combined to create the unparalleled splendor of the château of **Vaux-le-Vicomte.** Nicolas Fouquet, superintendent of finances for Louis XIV, inherited the property in 1641. In 1656 he commissioned Louis Le Vau to design a new château. More than 18,000 men were engaged in the construction of the vast, gray stone rectangular structure. The opulent interior decoration of the four corner pavilions and the oval pavilion on the garden façade was completed by Le Brun in 1661. André Lenôtre's formal garden at Vaux-le-Vicomte is one of the most beautiful in the world.

Fouquet's enjoyment of his new châ-

teau was painfully brief. Immediately following an elaborate inaugural reception in 1661, he was arrested and sentenced to life imprisonment by Louis XIV. The king then proceeded to employ Fouquet's architect, decorator, and landscape gardener to create the grandest of all châteaux — Versailles.

Selected Bibliography

Dunlop, Ian. *Versailles*. London: Hamish Hamilton, 1956.

Lefebvre, Georges. *The Coming of the French Revolution*. New York: Vintage Books, 1957.

Levron, Jacques. *Daily Life at Versailles in the Seventeenth Century*. London: George Allen & Unwin Ltd., 1968.

Levron, Jacques, and Van Der Kemp, Gerald. *Versailles*. Paris: Arthaud, 1957.

Mitford, Nancy. *Madame de Pompadour*. London: Hamish Hamilton, 1954.

————. *The Sun King*. New York: Harper & Row Publishers, 1966.

Nolhac, Pierre de. *La Résurrection de Versailles*. Paris: Librairie Plon, 1937.

————. *Versailles and the Trianons*. New York: Dodd Mead & Co., 1906.

Orlandi, Enzo. *The Life and Times of Louis XIV*. Translated by C. J. Richards. Philadelphia: Curtis Publishing Co., 1967.

Palacios, Alva Gonzalez. *The Age of Louis XV*. London: Paul Hamlyn, 1969.

Saint-Simon, Duc de. *Louis XIV at Versailles: A Selection of the Memoirs of the Duc de Saint-Simon*. Edited and translated by Desmond Flower. London: Folio Society, 1953.

Stevenson, Gertrude Scott, ed. and trans. *The Letters of Madame. Correspondence of Elizabeth-Charlotte of Bavaria*. 2 vols. New York: D. Appleton & Co., 1925.

Tocqueville, Alexis de. *The Old Regime and the French Revolution*. New York: Doubleday, 1955.

Ziegler, Gilette. *At the Court of Versailles*. Translated by Simon Watson Taylor. New York: E. P. Dutton, 1968.

Acknowledgments and Picture Credits

The Editors make grateful acknowledgment for the use of excerpted material from the following works:

The Adams Papers, Volume 4. Edited by Lyman H. Butterfield. Copyright 1961 by the Massachusetts Historical Society. The excerpt appearing on pages 146–47 is reproduced by permission of the Massachusetts Historical Society and the Belknap Press of Harvard University Press.

The Letters of Madame. Correspondence of Elizabeth-Charlotte of Bavaria, 2 vols. Edited and translated by Gertrude Scott Stevenson. Copyright 1925 by D. Appleton & Co. The excerpts appearing on pages 139–43 are reproduced by permission of Appleton-Century-Crofts, Inc.

Letters from Madame La Marquise de Sévigné. Selected and translated by Violet Hammersley. Copyright 1955 by Martin Secker & Warburg Ltd. The excerpt appearing on pages 138–39 is reproduced by permission of Martin Secker & Warburg Ltd.

The Papers of Benjamin Franklin, Volume 14. Edited by Leonard W. Labaree. Copyright 1970 by the American Philosophical Society. The excerpt appearing on page 145 is reproduced by permission of Yale University Press.

The Papers of Thomas Jefferson, Volume 12. Edited by Julian P. Boyd. Copyright 1955 by Princeton University Press. The excerpt appearing on pages 147–49 is reproduced by permission of Princeton University Press.

Versailles and the Trianons by Pierre de Nolhac. Copyright 1906 by Dodd Mead & Co. The excerpt appearing on page 160 is reproduced by permission of Dodd Mead & Co. and William Heinemann Ltd.

The Editors would like to express their particular appreciation to Gerald Van Der Kemp, curator of the Château de Versailles, for his generous cooperation, to Barbara Nagelsmith in Paris for her assistance in obtaining pictorial material, to Adam Woolfitt of London for his creative photography at the château, and to Thomas Froncek in New York who wrote the captions for this volume. In addition, the Editors would like to thank the following organizations and individuals:

Jane de Cabanyes, Madrid
Château de Versailles — Roland Bossard, Max Saltet
Marilyn Flaig, New York
Kate Lewin, Paris
Helen Benton Minnich, Minneapolis
Musées Nationaux, Paris — Anne-Marie Desaux, Beatrice de Boissason, Bernadette de Villedary
Susan Storer, New York

The title or description of each picture appears after the page number (boldface), followed by its location. Photographic credits appear in parentheses. The following abbreviations are used:

BN,P — Bibliothèque Nationale, Paris
V(MN) — Versailles (Musées Nationaux)
(AW) — (Adam Woolfitt)

ENDPAPERS The western and northern façades of Versailles from the northern gardens (AW) HALF TITLE Symbol designed by Jay J. Smith Studio FRONTISPIECE Chandeliers in the Opéra at Versailles (AW) **9** Stained-glass window in the chapel at Versailles. V(MN) **10–11** Plan of Versailles by Charbonnier and Delagrive, 1746. BN,P **12–13** Gilded shutters at Versailles (AW)

CHAPTER I **15** Keystone portrait from the western façade of Versailles (AW) **16–17** Tapestry of the wedding of Louis XIV and Marie Thérèse, June 9, 1660, by Henri Testelin. V(MN) **18** Pastel of Louis XIV by Charles Le Brun. Cabinet des Dessins, Louvre **19** Engraving of Vaux-le-Vicomte by Adam Perelle (Radio Times Hulton Library) **20** Drawing of a device for transporting orange trees, by Nicodemus Tessin. Nationalmuseum, Stockholm **21** Anonymous painting of Louis XIV in front of the Grotto of Thetis, 17th century. V(MN) **22** Engraving of the menagerie at Versailles by Adam Perelle. V(MN) **23** Engraving of Louise de La Vallière by H. Bonnart. BN,P **24** Portrait of Marie Thérèse and the dauphin by Pierre Mignard. Prado (David Manso Martin) **26–27** Painting of Versailles from the east in 1668, by Pierre Patel. V(MN) **28** Engraving of Molière's *La Princesse d'Élide* **29** Engraving of *L'Isle d'Alcine*. Both from Israel Silvestre's *Les Plaisirs de l'Isle Enchantée . . . à Versailles . . . L'Année 1664*. BN,P **30–31** Fireworks at Versailles on July 25, 1971 (AW)

CHAPTER II Keystone portrait from the western façade of Versailles (AW) **34–35** top and bottom left, The Chariot of Apollo at Versailles; right, The Fountain of Latona at Versailles (AW) **37** Portrait bust of Louis XIV by Giovanni Lorenzo Bernini. V(MN). **38–39** Painting of Jean Baptiste Colbert overseeing the building of Versailles, by Adam François Van der Meulen, *c.* 1678. Her Majesty the Queen, Copyright Reserved **40–41** Two woodcuts from Juan de La Quintinie's *Le Parfait Jardinier . . .*, 1695. Both, British Museum **42** The Queen's Staircase at Versailles. V(MN) **43** Painting of Mme. de Montespan and her children, after Pierre Mignard. V(MN) **44** Detail of a sketch for a tapestry showing Louis XIV visiting the Gobelin factory, by Charles Le Brun, *c.* 1672. Louvre **45** Sketch for the painting *Le Passage du Rhin*, by Charles Le Brun. Louvre **46** Pen and ink drawing of a façade at Marly by Charles Le Brun, *c.* 1679. Louvre **47** Painting of Marly from the north in 1724, by Pierre Denis Martin. V(MN)

CHAPTER III **49** Keystone portrait from the western façade of Versailles (AW) **50** top, Section of the stable at Versailles (AW); bottom, Painting of the forecourts and stables at Versailles by Jean Baptiste Martin, *c.* 1690. V(MN) **51** Relief of three horses from the arcade of the stable at Versailles (AW) **52** Engraving of the *Grand Lever* of Louis XIV, by Patas. BN,P **53** Engraving of the Galerie des Glaces at Versailles by Sebastien Le Clerc. BN,P **54–55** The Galerie des Glaces at Versailles. V(MN) **57** top, Engraving of ladies of the court in the fourth room; middle, Billiards playing in the third room. BN,P; bottom, Card playing in the second room. All from Antoine Trouvain's *Les Grands Appartements,* Paris, 1694–96; top and bottom, The Minnich Collection, Minneapolis Institute of Arts **58** Gardens at Versailles (AW) **59** Detail of a painting of the Fountain of Apollo by Jean Baptiste Martin, 1688. V(MN) **60** Anonymous engraving of the marriage of the dauphin in 1680. BN,P **61** Anonymous engraving of the birth of the dauphin's first child in 1682. BN,P **62** Painting of the dauphin and his family by Pierre Mignard, 1687. V(MN) **63** top, Portrait of Philippe, Duc d'Orléans, by Jean Nocret. Prado (David Manso Martin); bottom, Portrait of Elisabeth Charlotte of Bavaria, Duchesse d'Orléans, by Nicholas de Largillière. Musée Condé, Chantilly (Giraudon)

CHAPTER IV **65** Keystone portrait from the western façade of Versailles (AW) **66** Engraving of the water machine of Marly from Demortain's *Les Plans, Profiles et Elevations des Ville et Château de Versailles,* 1716. British Museum **67** Portrait of Louis XIV by Hyacinthe Rigaud. Louvre **68** Anonymous engraving of the revocation of the Edict of Nantes, 1685. BN,P **69** Anonymous engraving of Louis XIV receiving James II at Versailles in 1689. BN,P **70–71** top left, The Grand Trianon from the peristyle; bottom, The peristyle of the Grand Trianon from the staircase; top right, Detail of the entrance gate to the Grand Trianon (AW) **73** top, Portrait of Mme. de Maintenon by Pierre Mignard. Musée de Versailles (Bulloz); bottom, Portrait of the Duchesse de Bourgogne by Pierre Gobert. V(MN) **74** Anonymous engraving of the marriage of the Duc de Bourgogne and Marie Adélaïde of Savoy, on December 7, 1697. BN,P **75** Almanac engraving of the baptism of the Duc de Bretagne, June 25, 1704. BN,P **76** The chapel at Versailles. V(MN) **77** Miniature of Louis XIV at morning prayer in the chapel at Versailles. BN,P, Ms. Latin 9477, fol B.v **78** Anonymous engraving of Louis XIV on his deathbed, September 1, 1715. BN,P **79** Anonymous engraving of the funeral of Louis XIV, September 9, 1715. BN,P

Index